y Rockwell's
;Y RECIPES

- **Over** 200 tasty, allergy-free meals and snacks - all
  created with a **K.I.S.S.** *Keep It Simple, Sweetie*

- **Plus** - Timely tips and helpful hints on how to
  cope with an allergy-free diet - in & out of the kitchen.

ALL Recipes are Free of :

Milk Products: (casein, cheese, sour cream, non-fat
dry milk, whey or yogurt) **eggs, soy, peanuts, yeast,
refined sugars, preservatives, or colorings -** &
may be prepared with - or without - grains or gluten -
*Amaranth, barley, buckwheat, corn, kamut, oats, millet,
quinoa, rice, rye, spelt, teff or wheat* - are all
optional   ingredients.

Please Note -

Ideas in this publication are for information only, and not to be taken as medical advice. Consult your health professional before making dietary changes. See back pages for help finding a physician in your area who treats food sensitivities and allergies.

On-site Training for Health Professionals & the General Public; Workshops; Cooking Classes; Telephone Counseling; Lectures and Support Groups -
F.A.A.S.T.- Food Allergy - Addiction Support Teams
Send a #10 SASE for a free copy of Sally's newsletter, *ALLERGY ALERT.*

Other self-help books available: Calcium Without the Cow • Coping with Candida Cookbook • The Rotation Game • Illustrated Guide Books • Audio and Video Cassette Tapes & more. See back pages for more information.

Dr. Sally J. Rockwell, Nutritionist
4703 Stone Way N.   Seattle, Washington 98103
Telephone: (206) 547-1814   FAX (206) 547-7696

About the Author

No - It's Not "All In Your Mind" - Yes - There's Life After Allergies -

Dr. Sally's personal victory over addictions and health problems launched her crusade to help others. She's overcome a long history of health problems* - alcoholism, compulsive eating, bingeing, obesity, prescription drug abuse and more - by researching a wide variety of approaches to healing. THE most helpful was - and still is - avoiding allergenic and binge-inducing foods.

Her colorful past and a quick wit make her a popular guest on local and national radio and television talk shows. She travels far & wide, lecturing, teaching & conducting workshops.

Professional Affiliations -
American Academy of Environmental Medicine; Am. Academy of Otolaryngic Allergy; Am. Holistic Medical Association; Center for Science in the Public Interest; Pan American Allergy Society; Society for Nutrition Education; Washington State Food and Nutrition Council; Well Mind Association & others.

Honors -   Who's Who of American Women, 1988-89
Who's Who in the West, 1989-90

Dr. Sally is continually developing *Self-Help Resources* - books, games, tapes - to support & empower you - help you put some fun back into your meals and into your life!

*Sally looks at "*problems*" as *challenges.* - puzzles waiting to be solved.

What's Wrong With Me?

My doctors all said - *Your test results show nothing physically wrong with you ..., it's all in your mind...."*
In my long search for answers, here's a sampling of the workshops, encounter groups, retreats, etc. , which I experienced *before* I changed my diet:

Workshops From A To Z -

A. Anger, Aerobics, Autogenics, Acupuncture, Assertive Training, Amphetamines, Allergy Injections
B. Biofeedback, Bioenergetics, Bladder Repair
C. Chiropractic, Colonics, Counseling
D. Dental Work -TMJ & mercury removal, Dianetics, Dance
E. E.S.T. Graduate, Eye Exercises, *E.P.D.*
F. Feldenkrais
G. Gestalt, Years Of Gestalt!
H. Hypnosis, Homeopathy, Hands-On-Healing, Hysterectomy
I. Iridology, Ionizers, Immune Therapy
J. Jungian Therapy
K. Kinesiology
L. Love, Unconditional Love, Letting Go, Lifespring
M. Meditation, Massage Training, Mega-Vitamins & Minerals
N. Neurolinguistics, Needless Surgeries
O. Orthoptics, Orthopedics, On Course, O.A.
P. Past Life Regression, Psychologists, Psychiatrists
Q. Quercitin, Quaalude
R. Reflexology, Rebirthing, RET, Rolfing (16 Sessions)
S. Shiatsu, Stress Management, Screaming, Self Esteem
T. Transactual Analysis, Touch For Health, Tai Chi
U. Uterus Removed, Urine Injections
V. Veins Stripped, Valium
W. Wailing & Wellness Workshops
X. X-rays
Y. Yoga, Yelling
Z. Zen

When I removed the coffee and junk food from my life - a *miracle* happened - I no longer felt *crazy*

Sick & Tired
of feeling
Sick & Tired?

What You're Eating
May Be What's Eating You

In 1975, my latest psychiatrist (one of dozens), Karl Hummiston M.D., suggested I take the coffee and white sugar out of my life. **WOW !** I began to function. Next, I began to explore food allergies. By following the elimination and rotation diet system, I identified the foods that were making me sick - *and causing my bingeing and over-eating.* I became myself again! My head cleared up, the *brain fog* lifted and my energy returned.

I entered college for the first time in my life as a single parent, at age 42, earned a BS in Nutrition at the University of Washington; and completed my Ph.D. in Clinical Nutrition in 1995 from The Union Institute, Cincinnati, Ohio.

How could anything as simple as changing your diet make such a big difference in how you feel? Just try it and see for yourself.

Have you been through the regular medical channels, been pronounced "healthy" and you're still experiencing unpleasant symptoms? Then try the Elimination diet for just five days. Symptoms associated with CFS, Fibromyalsia, Interstitial cystitis, Digestive Disorders, Depression, IBS, bowel disturbances and loss of energy - *are often related to food allergies (or sensitivities) and candida yeast overgrowth* and may improve, or even disappear.

I want everyone to feel just half as energetic and happy as I do. *If I can do it, SO CAN YOU !*

Why not try this drug-free diet NOW?

Sally

A Giant Hug And A Thank You to all of you who have written to me. I love hearing about your favorite recipes - what works - what doesn't - and where you need more help. In response to those requests, I have developed several new books and tapes.

Why? Because I want to help everyone feel as vibrant and full of energy as I finally do, and it's entirely possible; by identifying the foods that don't agree with you, and then following this *Rotation Diet Plan* for a while.

What Does The Rotation Diet Do? It eliminates the foods that may be making you sick & tired, creates variety, will reduce or eliminate your current food sensitivities and keep new allergies from developing.

Can I Ever Have Wheat Again? Giving up your favorite foods is not forever, just until the symptoms subside. You can begin to add back the omitted foods in about three to six months, after the immune system has a chance to rest and rejuvenate. With the alarmingly rapid increase in Immune System Diseases, the stronger we can become, the healthier we'll be.

What About Vitamins? Do take vitamin C daily, plus a good hypo allergenic vitamin/mineral capsule and essential fatty acids (EFA's), like those found in flax oil, vegetable oils like olive - black currant - safflower - sunflower - sesame - evening primrose oil and fish oils. Cod liver oil is good for you but it's NOT the same thing.

How much Vit. C.? Start with a small amount of Buffered C (contains calcium, potassium & magnesium) - 1/8 tsp., 4X a day - in water, between meals - gradually increase the dose, just a little at a time, until you reach *bowel tolerance*: 'Til you get a rumbly gut, soft stool or diarrhea, then reduce the dose.

My doctor says there's no such thing as _food allergy._ Space doesn't permit me to elaborate on that right now. Whether you say _allergy, sensitivity or hypersensitivity,_ the treatment is the same: Eliminate the suspect food, rotate all other foods, then reintroduce.

What's an Elimination Diet? You eliminate, or avoid, any food that you may be allergic to.

Where Do I Start? If you have my _Rotation Game_, take out the colored _Master Chart_ and cross out the foods you will be avoiding. This book is a companion to the _Game._ Don't have the chart? Then turn to the first page of each colored section in this book and draw a pencil line through the foods you are avoiding. What's not crossed out is what's left to eat. _What you see is what you get._ Use these pages for your shopping list.

Do I Have To Rotate?
No. _HOWEVER,_ If you are allergic to wheat, and you start eating rice every day, you will most likely become allergic to rice, or any other grain you eat daily.

Repetitive eating is a major cause of food intolerance-eating the same foods day after day after day. That's why wheat, milk, eggs, corn, soy, peanuts, refined sugars and yeast - foods we eat daily - are common allergens.

How Do I _Rotate?_
Eat a food only once every four days. But, you don't have to think about how to rotate, I've done the thinking and planning for you! These recipes and menu ideas are actually PRE-ROTATED. My Game and recipe book make it easy and fun.

What are the colored pages for?
Each colored section represents a different day. Day 1 is
the green section - *Green Day* , Day 2 is the yellow
section - *Yellow Day*, Day 3 is *Blue Day* and
Day 4 is *Red Day*.

The fun comes in with the color coding. Imagine each
food container in your kitchen having a color-coded label
- either green - Day 1; yellow - Day 2, and so on. By using
colored stickers and twist ties (included in the *Game*) all
the food containers will be identified as belonging to a
specific day. So each shelf in the cupboard, refrigerator
and freezer has food containers marked either green,
yellow, blue or red.

When preparing a meal for day 1, simply reach for the
food containers with the green labels or green rubber
bands on them and start cooking. Prepare several days
snacks in advance, label with the appropriate color, and
the family can help themselves each day. Get the kids
involved, they love to *sticke*r things.

How To Make The Family Independent. Purchase
4 colored bows, one for each day, and fasten to a
magnet. On Day 1, green Day, stick the green bow on the
refrigerator. By matching colors, they can SEE what to eat
each day. Or, place a colored rubber band (a loose one)
around a pre-schoolers wrist and they can choose by
matching colored snacks without asking "WHAT CAN I
EAT, MOMMY? I'M HUNGRY"

"But I Already Have Too Much to Do." Take your
time. Start with the color coding a little at a time. The
object is to get into a simple routine which will reduce
stress; not add another stress into your life.

Allergies & Candida Yeast - What's the Connection? Briefly - Candida yeast overgrowth can be a major contributing factor in food allergies, and vice versa.

Why? The toxins (poisons) produced by the yeast overwhelm our immune systems and allergies begin to develop (or vice versa). A high-sugar intake &/or poor diet leads to vitamin and mineral deficiencies which reduce our body's ability to heal itself and our health begins to deteriorate. We develop more and more unusual, seeming unrelated symptoms. When we get the Candida yeast under control, we lighten the load on our immune systems, and our food & chemical sensitivities begin to improve.

What Do I Do if I Suspect Candida Yeast Problems? Try the simple Cave Man diet plan for 10 days and note any changes in your mental and physical functions.

What's the Cave Man Diet?
Lots and lots of vegetables: Every way except fried. Raw is best, of course, then steamed or stir fried, soups and stews; frozen is okay. Lots of beans and peas, root vegetables; and some protein foods: Such as fish, shellfish, chicken, turkey, rabbit, nuts and seeds. See colored pages for specific foods allowed each day.

Avoid: Eggs, refined sugars, breads or pastas, all milk products and yeasty-fermented foods. This Cave Man plan *starves out the yeast* (and also helps detect the foods you may be allergic to).

What's the difference in the Cave Man Diet and the Elimination Diet? The Cave Man Diet has no fruit the first five days; the Elimination Diet includes all fruit except citrus (oranges, grapefruit, lemons and limes).

How Do I Know If I Have Allergies?
Avoid the suspect foods, then add them back one at a time, and your body will tell you. When your symptoms have calmed down, usually after five to ten days (sometimes longer), then begin to add foods back into your diet.

Re-introduce a food by eating it by itself, plain, in the morning before eating anything else. No symptoms? It's probably safe now. If you get symptoms, avoid the food another month. If no reaction, then incorporate it into your rotation plan, eating it once every four days.

Keep a thorough record of all you eat and drink, plus note all symptoms, mental and physical: aches, pains, skin rashes, itchy ears or rectum, muscle soreness, stiffness Include attitude changes such as more patience, calmer, stronger sense of self esteem, thinking clearer, require less sleep, etc. (See detailed instructions in my *Rotation Game* or *Guide Book #2)*

What's the Allergy - Addiction Connection?
We can actually become addicted to foods we are allergic to, and if we don't get a `fix', that is, have that specific food daily, we may go through withdrawal symptoms. Feeling worse for the first 3 to 5 days on an elimination diet is normal, but then, little by little the old complaints should start to disappear.

How Harmful is Cheating on the Diet?
Almost all of us slip off the diet occasionally, just get back on it the very next day. Be nice to yourself! Be your own best friend. What's harmful is beating yourself up for indulging and playing 'kick me'. Relax, you're human - we all go astray occasionally.

How Far Can I Go Off the Diet Without Destroying All the Good I've Done? I don't know.
You'll find out just how far you can go after slipping once or twice, just get back on it *immediately*.

How Does Stress Affect My Health?

A major contributing factor to our dis-eases are dis-stresses. Selye describes stress as "The bodies struggle to adapt to a *noxious agent . . .*" That *noxious agent* may be an associate, a family member (ooops- sad but true), polluted air and water, artificial lighting, preservatives or colorings in food, candida yeast infestation, food allergies or *too strict a diet.*.

Ideal "Perfect" Diet versus Real "do-able" Diets

Ideal diets tend to be rigid, but the closer you can follow one, the sooner you'll get well. They look wonderful on paper, but are not always do-able. If the diet is too strict, it may add stress to an already stressed-out person. In my experience, *stricter the diet, the sooner one quits* - then begins to feel guilty and resentful. Guilt and stress are counter productive and slow down the healing process. So let's aim for a more *realistic* approach.

The Real Diet is the one you can live with over time and still achieve your goals. It's practical, flexible, easier on you, your family and friends; you'll stay on it long enough to get well. AND - you'll retain (or regain) your sanity, which is no small feat in this day and age.

What's an ideal meal? A wide variety of organically grown, raw or barely steamed vegetables, legumes, fresh fruits, sprouts, fish, poultry, raw nuts and raw seeds, whole, stone ground grains; served in a *loving and relaxed* atmosphere, totally free of stress, conflict or pollution . The *perfect meal* is a goal to aim for; so do whatever you can - whenever you can - towards that goal It's worth it!

Notes -

Fast Food Eateries

Bad News: they're here to stay.
Good News: Healthy foods are available at some of them.
Better News: Healthier fast-food eateries are springing up everywhere.

Fish & Chips - Find one in your area with 'chunks' of fish rather than flat fillets, so when the coating is peeled off you can find the fish. A salad bar would be best, of course, however, if one is unavailable, a side of cole slaw and a *few* french fried potatoes are okay.

Baked Potatoes - Wendy's, and I hope other places in the country, have hot baked potatoes with lots of toppings available. An excellent choice is lots of vegetables from the salad bar, or salsa, or chili on top.

Salad bars - If I have a choice, I avoid the regular *head* or *iceberg* lettuce. Romaine or leaf lettuce are less likely to have been dipped in some sort of anti-browning (and Lord only knows what that may be) solution. I also look for spinach, cabbage, raw veggies like broccoli, cauliflower, carrots, celery, sprouts, radishes, olives, onions; fresh fruit, refried beans, guacamole, sunflower seeds.

Salad Dressings - oil and lemon or vinegar dressing is the best choice, Italian is next; the others are usually full of sugars and food colorings. Mayonnaise is fine; it is not a dairy product. It does contain eggs, but eggs are not dairy, they don't come from cows. Low-fat mayonnaise's are usually thickened with wheat or corn starch - I avoid them.

Condiments: Ketchup is one-third (1/3) sugar, tartar sauce is a better choice; mustard is great.

Mexican -*Taco Time, Macheezmo Mouse,* (best choices),*Taco Bell,* etc. Peel a burrito and eat the middle only, discard the shell if you are allergic to wheat. Tostadas are flat corn tortillas with beans, chicken or meat, lettuce and cheese piled on top. I order it with beans and chicken only. It's easier to eat than a taco. Avoid the corn tortilla on the bottom if you're allergic to corn. Chili is usually okay and so is a Taco Salad. Ask them to "hold the cheese and sour cream". Use salsa or guacamole instead.

Pizza Parlors - Not much available if allergic to milk and wheat. Eat the topping only, not the crust. Have a side order of meatballs or salad if available.

Fried Chicken - Peel the coating off the chicken. A side of beans, three bean salad, coleslaw or potatoes are wiser choices than biscuits, muffins or gravy.

Burgers - Hooray for veggie, fish or chicken burgers! If not available, eat the middle of a *well done* hamburger or a cheese burger. If allergic to wheat, any type of salad or vegetable you can order on the side is a wiser choice than buns, or bread or biscuits.

Convenience Stores - Warm up a burrito in the microwave and eat the middle with a spoon. If allergic to wheat and dairy, packaged nuts, popcorn, peanuts, sunflower seeds or beef jerky - are emergency suggestions that would be better choices than a Danish roll, donut or candy.

What About Socializing? Dinner Parties?

Yes, you can enjoy an evening with friends. Good friends understand (or will try at least) when hearing you need to avoid sauces, casseroles and noodles. Tell them baked or sautéed fish, roast beef, turkey, baked potato, vegetables and green salad will be just fine.

There are times when one must be a bit devious and clever, depending on your relationship with the host and hostess. Strangers, or those who don't understand food allergies, don't need to know. Eat before you go if you don't know the menu in advance. Offer to bring a "new" dip recipe. Then, of course, take along the dippers (raw vegetables, potato chips, carrot chips, etc.) Fresh roasted nuts are always welcome snack food. Bring your own mineral water.

If you find yourself dealing with an 'alcohol pusher' or a person who thinks allergies are not real, cross your fingers and tell them that the medication you're taking doesn't mix with wine. Or, tell them you're "pre-diabetic" (just another way of saying 'hypo-glycemic'). It's unfortunate but not unusual for medications to be acceptable while allergies are not understood at all. Attempting to explain your special diet may prove to be a waste of time. *Don't feel like you have to apologize and don't be afraid to say "NO thank you."*

If you're not up on it . . . you're down on it.
In other words if they don't understand a health condition, or they know nothing about it, they often assume it's *psychosomatic.* and label you as a hypochondriac.

Dining Out

The fun and relaxation of dining out may far outweigh the nuisance of an allergic reaction. Choose a restaurant that offers some of the following foods, whenever possible.

Choose baked, broiled or sautéed fish, poultry or meats without sauces. It is usually acceptable when dining out to ask for sauces and salad dressings on the side, then simply don't use it. If nothing appeals to you on the main entrees, order from the appetizer or a la carte sections. I often make a meal out of 2 small salads and a baked potato.

A seafood cocktail (sauce on the side), salad: spinach, tossed green, Caesar, coleslaw or sliced tomato, with dressing on the side - add a hot vegetable - for a well rounded meal, satisfying meal.

Breakfast is the most difficult restaurant meal if allergic to wheat, milk and eggs. Fresh fruit, oatmeal and hash browns are good choices. Combine side dishes like eggs, ground beef patty, ham, sausage or bacon (unless severely sensitive to preservatives) - whatever fits into your diet.

Ask if they have any lunch items readily available - like a tuna mixture, or sliced turkey, or chili or soup, coleslaw, perhaps a salad (if the chef is congenial). Think positive and ask, but don't count on it.

Need more ideas? Send for my booklet - *Meals and Snacks for Travel, Trail and Packs*

Brown Bag Lunch Ideas

Plan ahead. Avoid early-morning hassles.
Assemble lunches right after dinner, while the kitchen is still in a mess. Place leftovers in small containers and refrigerate or freeze right away. See recipes for *Veggie Burgers* and pages on *Crock Pot Cooking* for time-saving ideas.

1. Maintain a supply of novelty napkins, utensils and small containers. Add special notes, jokes or riddles frequently.

2. Handy supplies include: Wide mouth thermos (vacuum bottles) are ideal for hot cereals, chili, soup, stew, etc. Hint: Stick an 'acceptable' hot dog in thermos, cover with very hot water. Also good for perishable cold dishes, sandwich fillings, salads, and puddings. Cold pack by packing 'blue ice' in the bottom of the lunch bag, or use an old flat plastic lotion bottle. Fill bottle 3/4 full of water, freeze and place in plastic bag and seal.

3. Include foods for children that you *know* they enjoy. Do the testing at home.

4. Keep an SOS lunch at school or office for emergencies. Small containers of sugar-free juices, Nutri-ola bars and sugar-free fruit roll-ups are always good, beef or turkey jerky, small bags of nuts or seeds, crackers and nut butters, cans of sardines, or home canned foods and other non-perishables will be welcome. If a freezer is available make use of it also.

5. Toss in extras occasionally for your child to share - **not** trade.

6. Whip up an extra batch of pancakes or flatbreads ahead of time; ready to fill with a variety of spreads. Pack separately when using moist fillings.

7. Pack lettuce and cabbage leaves separately to avoid wilting.

8. Freeze small quantities of meats, poultry, crackers, spreads, etc. and package individually. Put these into the lunch bag at the last minute, they will be fresh and cold but thawed by lunch time.

9. See recipes and menu plans for a variety of fillings, salads and hot or cold one- dish meals. This variety will keep lunch interesting.

10. Take one afternoon a week (or a month) to bake acceptable muffins, cookies, pancakes, crackers, flat breads, etc.

11. Package several small batches of nuts and dried fruit - *trail mix* - *for each of the four days.*

12. Ask the lunch eaters to plan their own menus occasionally and to give you their ideas.

13. Un-sandwich items, like celery, cabbage and lettuce leaves, cucumber or jicama slices, all work great for scooping up or enfolding sandwich fillings.

14. Use sprouts for fun and variety. Learn to sprout your own. See *Complete Guide To Sprouting* in my *Coping With Candida Cookbook.*

SANDWICH FILLINGS

Stir your imagination and get the creative juices (and the digestive juices) flowing.

Anything edible can be sliced, mashed or chopped - used 'as is' - or combined and spread on toast, a flat bread, tortilla, pancake, waffle, muffin, cracker or any of the vegetables on the previous page.

See the first page of each colored section for specific food choices.

Fillings: Mix hummus, tahini, nut butters, mayonnaise, mustard, or tartar sauce with all sorts of chopped vegetables, sprouts, nuts or seeds.

Nut Butters can be used as is, thinned with fruit juices, mixed with chopped nuts or seeds, chopped dried fruit, mixed with creamy tofu (soy) or salad dressings (see recipes), or mayonnaise (if tolerated).

Combine any of the above with preservative-free luncheon meats, chopped, cooked meats, poultry, shrimp or seafood, tuna, mashed sardines, mashed beans, olives, pickles, onions, sprouts, radishes, etc.

Add: Finely grated parsnips, carrots, turnips, jicama, coconut, or mashed avocado. Spread, stack or roll up and enjoy.

You'll create some winning combinations and some that even the dog won't touch. That's all a part of the learning process -- just like learning a new language -- it gets easier with time and practice.

What's Left To Eat If I Can't Have Wheat?

Good News! Would you believe that most of the following are available as whole grains, flours, starches, noodles and various shaped pastas? Amaranth, barley, buckwheat, corn, kamut, millet, oats, quinoa, rice, wild rice, rye, spelt, teff, sorghum, chestnuts, potatoes, beans (garbanzo flour is nice), lentils, and more. See back pages for resources and ordering information.

What Is Gluten Intolerance?

 Gluten is a protein fraction found in wheat*, spelt*, triticale*, kamut*, rye*, oats*, barley*, teff* and millet* (in descending order). Those who have celiac spru (gluten intolerance) are unable to digest gluten. It inflames their intestine and destroys the brush border villi which line the intestine wall, sort of like a shag carpet. These villi produce digestive enzymes and help us to absorb our nutrients. Celiacs and gluten-sensitive folks get sick and under-nourished when they consume grains which contain gluten.

Rice and corn are gluten free; amaranth, quinoa and buckwheat have a different type of gluten that doesn't seem to bother most celiacs. These grains are considered *essentially gluten-free* (EGF**).

Amaranth and Quinoa are biologically classified as seeds, and were staple foods of the Aztec Indians. They're grown organically and contain more calcium, protein, fiber, and amino acids lysine and methionine than most grains.

* Contain gluten.   **EGF, Marge Jones, *Super Foods*.

What are Guar Gum and Xanthan Gum?

Xanthan Gum and guar gum thicken liquids without cooking, and are *fun* to play with in the kitchen. A small amount added to any liquid turns it into a creamy smooth 'mouth feel' like rich ice cream.

Meat or fish drippings (au jus) turn into fluffy sauces and gravies; fruit juice transforms into pudding or gelatin-like dessert; nut milk and carob powder looks and tastes like chocolate pudding; salad dressings thicken so they don't separate. Foods remain creamy after thawing without curdling.

These gums do not mix well by hand; a rotary mixer, blender or food processor is necessary for best results. Xanthan gum is an excellent substitute for gluten when attempting to bake with gluten-free flours. See recipes.

Xanthan is a tiny microorganism called Xanthomonas Campestris It grows a special protective coating which is removed by a chemical process, dried and milled to form a powder. These polysaccharides are not readily absorbed in the human intestine. Approximately 8 calories per tablespoon.

Guar is a vegetable gum in the legume, or bean family.
Notes -

Thickeners & Binders
Use in place of wheat or other grains

Hot Sauces:
To thicken gravies, white sauce, puddings, and so on, Corn Starch, Potato Starch, Tapioca, Amaranth, quinoa, Arrowroot, Agar (seaweed), Bean Flours - and any of the other flours mentioned on previous pages.

Dissolve in cold water, mix thoroughly. To prevent unsightly lumps, add to hot liquids slowly; stirring constantly until thickened.

Hot or Cold:
None of these gums require heat to thicken.
Guar gum, pectin, gum arabic, xanthan gum, guar gum, locust bean gum can be used in place of wheat or eggs for binding seeds, nuts and starches that crumble or fall apart when baked.

Root Vegetables:
Carrots, parsnips, potatoes, turnips, squashes, etc., can thickening stews, soups and gravies, just cook, mash and stir 'em in.

Guess What? A Flour Can Be Made From Almost Any Starchy Food.

Flours can be made from any starchy vegetable, root vegetable, tuber, legume or grain.

Legume (bean) Flours may be made by using a seed grinder, blender or food processor - use according to manufacturer's directions. Sort for stones, wash, dry thoroughly, then process until a fine powder is achieved.

Flours, con't --

Starchy Vegetable Flours from squash, pumpkins, yams, sweet potatoes, white potatoes or carrots may be made by peeling and cutting vegetable into chunks, drying them in a food dehydrator or in a very slow oven. When thoroughly dry, grind until a fine powder or desired consistency is achieved.

All Flours: Label and store in airtight containers.

A Nut or Seed Meal is a flour made from nuts or seeds, and may be substituted for any flour. A *thickener* or starch acts like a glue, and is usually necessary to prevent the finished product from crumbling and improve the texture. Use the same directions as given for *Legume (bean) Flours.*

Baking Tips - Be aware that "alternative" flours are usually coarser than wheat flour and may require more liquid than the original recipe calls for.

Do mix with a liquid ahead of time, let mixture stand for several hours or overnight for a lighter, more desirable finished product. Add baking powder just before cooking, for it loses it's potency after being mixed with liquid.

My illustrated *Guide Book #6, Baking Tips and Tricks*, is helpful if you are experiencing the dreaded "soggy muffin middle syndrome" and other such frustrations.

Flour Substitutions

When the recipe calls for *1 Cup of White (wheat) Flour* - use:
- 1/2 cup arrowroot or tapioca with 1/2 cup of another flour or nut meal
- 7/8 cup buckwheat or amaranth flour
- 3/4 cup cornstarch or 7/8 cup corn flour or 1 cup of cornmeal.
- 5/8 cup potato flour or 3/4 cup potato starch.
- 3/4 cup oat flour or 1-1/2 cups rolled oats (ground).
- 3/4 cup rice flour, soy, barley, millet, or bean flours.

Non-Bread Bread Substitutes
Foods that can be rolled, stacked, filled, dipped or stuffed can take on new and ingenious shapes. In addition to these recipes *If tolerated in your diet* keep on hand - corn chips, rye crisp, rice crackers or rice cakes, oat cakes.

Vegetables (raw or cooked) are very popular dippers, such as celery, carrots, cauliflower, broccoli, turnips, rutabagas, parsnips, green pepper strips, cucumber slices, zucchini strips, jicama slices, potato chips,

There are also some vegetables, which make wonderful salads or meals themselves when 'stuffed', favorites are: red or green peppers, avocados, scooped out zucchini, acorn squash shells, baked potatoes, artichokes, tomatoes, cucumber *boats*, hard boiled eggs, lettuce and cabbage leaves. The only limits are your imagination and food allergies!

Pancakes, Flatbreads, Tortillas, Crepes -

What's the difference?

In one form for the other, they are the staple foods of people all over the world. The basic ingredients are quite simple: *some type of starch or flour and a liquid.* Optional ingredients are eggs, leavenings (yeast, baking powder or baking soda) a sweetener, nuts, seeds, fruit and all types of seasonings.

In other words 'anything goes', depending on your taste buds, ethnic preferences, whether or not it will be used for breakfast, lunch or dinner, or even dessert.

The typical American staple is a large, fluffy loaf of bread, made from less-that-healthy, over processed white flour. We slice it, toast it, spread it or stack it into sandwich type finger foods. It's so soft it rarely needs chewing, just squish it around in the mouth and swallow. (No wonder we're getting so sickly).

When we can no longer eat the grains that are used to make a fluffy loaf of sliced bread, what can we do? Pout? (Well, actually, most of us do go through a prolonged 'poor me' syndrome). Starve? Do without? No, we make different shapes with different sources of flours. Instead of slicing - make flat 'slices' (pancakes), spread with a filling and roll into finger food (like a jelly roll), or we can stack them with all sorts of fillings in between, like sandwiches.

Play with this flat bread recipe and prepare several different kinds; one from each of flours you can tolerate.

FLAT BREADS

Pre-heat oven to 400° F.   Make sure it's hot.

Flat Breads can be made with any flour, with or without gluten. They're like *tortillas.*

1 cup flour - buckwheat, amaranth, teff, quinoa
        millet, rice, etc. (any flour except potato)
1/2 tsp. baking soda or baking powder
1/2 cup water
2 tsp. oil
(You'll need 1/3 - 2/3 cup extra flour for kneading)

Sift the dry ingredients together. **Mix** oil and water together, then add to dry ingredients. Work together with a fork, and then with your hands - knead - roll into a ball. **Divide** into 6-8 smaller balls - pat flat. **Dust** each ball with flour, place between waxed paper sheets and roll to about 1/8" flat with a floured rolling pin (or glass jar). **Turn** over frequently; use enough flour to prevent sticking. Dampen kitchen counter so waxed paper won't slide around. Pour some oil in your hands and oil each bread.
Lightly oil a frying pan or griddle (or use a non-stick spray)

Put one flatbread at a time on the hot pan - 15-20 seconds on each side, place immediately into the oven - 3 minutes on each side. Enjoy hot; or cool, place in plastic bags & refrigerate or freeze. Great for sandwiches & snacks. *When the mood strikes - prepare several batches - mess up the kitchen all at once*

I modified a Marg Jones recipe, thanx Marg.

BREADINGS AND CRACKER CRUMBS
Toppings & coatings for baked or fried foods

Replace *bread or cracker crumbs* with purchased, or your own home made cracker crumbs, see recipes in each colored section. Use for coatings and for toppings.

Crumble rice cakes, rye crisp, corn chips, potato chips; or the Chex cereals - rice wheat, corn; Natural foods stores have amaranth, kamut, spelt, millet, quinoa cereals; or toast and crumble any bread - spelt, kamut, rice, pure rye, wheat, corn bread, leftover falafel, whatever you can find (or make yourself) - and use them on the appropriate days.

Grind any nut or seed into a meal.
Sesame seeds are a good coating for liver or chicken, all nuts work quite nicely - just moisten the food and dredge in coating mix.

Other coatings to try - dry, minced onion is an excellent coating for liver - yum! Potato flour, or instant mashed potato mix; dry, shredded coconut; dry falafel mix is terrific on fish. Bake or fry foods as usual. Just use your imagination, let me know what combinations you discover.

Hint -
Baking is preferred over frying, but this cookbook is to help you through the 'crisis' of learning how to rotate your foods, not to teach basic nutrition . . . that will come later when you're feeling well enough to think about more than just *"What in the world can I eat today?"*

EGG SUBSTITUTES

1 whole egg =	*2 tablespoons liquid +* 2 tablespoons flour + 1/2 tablespoon oil + 1/2 teaspoon baking powder
1 egg =	*1 tablespoon ground flax* or psyllium seed and 3 tablespoons of water
1 egg =	*2 tablespoons of apricot* mixture (see below)
1 egg =	*2 tablespoons water +* 2 teaspoons baking powder

Apricot Mixture (Egg Substitute)

1 cup dried apricots (most dried fruits work well)
Cover with boiling water, let stand until soft. Puree in
blender. Cover, store in refrigerator.

Egg White (substitute)
1 tablespoon plain unflavored gelatin. Dissolve gelatin in
1 tablespoon of water. Whip; chill, and whip again.
(Eloise Kailin, M.D.)

E ner-G Foods Egg Replacer: **Hint -** mix with water & let
stand 10 minutes before using for best results.

Order from: Ener-G Foods. Box 24724, Seattle, Washington,
981214.

VINEGAR SUBSTITUTES

Vinegar comes from fermenting a combination of molds and liquids (fruit juice, grain mixture, wine, cider, malt). Vinegar substitutions: lemon juice, lime juice, unsweetened cranberry juice or dilute Vitamin C (ascorbic acid) - mix 1 teaspoon in 1/4 cup of water.

LEAVENINGS

What's a leavening? A substance that creates bubbles in the batter or dough, and makes baked goods light and airy. Baking powder is part acid and part alkaline, and when mixed together in a liquid, it foams, or bubbles. Baking soda is alkaline, and foams best when mixed with an acid, like lemon juice, sour milk or Vitamin C crystals.
Yeast works the best; It feeds on the sugars and burps out gas, or bubbles. It's more labor-intensive; and tends to be allergenic, so I don't use it in any of my recipes.

Baking Powder #1
1 part potassium bicarbonate
2 parts cream of tartar
2 parts any starch - like arrowroot, rice flour, etc.
Mix thoroughly and store in a covered container.

Baking Powder #2   Equals 1 tsp. baking powder
1/2 teaspoon baking soda
1 teaspoon cream of tartar
Add to liquid just before baking. Good for muffins.

Baking Powder #3
1/4 teaspoon baking soda
1/2 tsp. any acid - lemon or lime juice, cream of tartar or Vit C - (ascorbic acid).

Sample Menus - Ideas To Get You Started

Fish may be eaten daily, as long as it's a different fish each day.

See colored pages for recipes

Monday	Tuesday
Day 1 (Green)	Day 2 (Yellow)

Breakfast

Eggs or
Sesame pancakes
  w. honey
Applesauce
Apple juice
Soy milk

Breakfast

Rice cereal
Veggie Patti
Rice muffins
Orange slices
Rice milk

Snacks

Broccoli, radishes,
Apples, Melons
Berries, Grapes
Bean Dip
Munchies #1
Nut Butter Cookies

Snacks

Carrots, bell peppers,
  Raw mushrooms
  Rice Cakes

Munchies #2
Herbal tea, juice

Lunch

Split Pea Soup
Arrowroot crackers
Raw vegetables
Pickles
Grapes

Lunch

Turkey salad
Turkey - rice soup
Rice cakes
Carrot sticks

Dinner

Chili w/ground beef or
Baked Chicken
Baked Yam
Marinated veggie salad

Muffins
Nut Bread #1

Dinner

Stuffed peppers
  w. rice & turkey
Grated carrot salad
Almond vegetables
Rice Cakes
Baked potato
Nut Bread #2

Sample Menus - Ideas To Get You Started

Fish may be eaten daily, as long as it's a different fish each day.

See colored pages for recipes

Wednesday
Day 3 (Blue)

Pork sausage or ham
Nut bread
Pears, Nut milk
Pineapple Juice
Melon Slices

Snacks
Radishes, cauliflower,
zucchini, olives
Pears, pineapple, melon
Figs, Currants
Munchies #3
Nut Butter Cookies #3

Lunch
Minestrone soup, p.108
or bean soup
Falafel
Marinated veggies

See Snacks Above

Dinner
Pork stir fry
Zucchini, cauliflower,
leeks, peas
Spinach salad
Falafel Squares
Nut Butter Cookies

Thursday
Day 4 (Red)

Granola (oats), Banana
Cashew Muffins & Cashew Butter
Maple Syrup
Cashew milk
Grapefruit or Tomato juice

Snacks
Celery, tomatoes, bell
   peppers w/dip (see
   salad dressing)
   Banana, Nectarine
Munchies #4
Corn chips, popcorn
Nut Butter Cookies #4

Lunch
Vegetable barley soup
Slice Avocado,
Corn Bread
Celery Sticks

See Snacks Above

Dinner
Rabbit stew or Fish
Stuffed Celery
Tomatoes & eggplant
Baked Sweet Potato
Green salad
Muffins or rolls

Day 1

Green Day

FOODS FOR DAY 1

Strictly optional - Just ignore what you don't like. Remember -- Day 1 and Day 3 foods are interchangeable.

PROTEIN:
Fish may be eaten daily as long as a different fish is selected each day. Chicken & eggs, Goose & eggs; Beef (veal, liver, organ meats, etc.); Mussels, escargot, clams.

LEGUME FAMILY: Kidney, soy, lima beans, all beans.
NUTS & OILS: Filberts, sesame seeds, soy nuts, walnuts

GRAINS, FLOURS & THICKENERS:
Buckwheat, quinoa, soy, tofu, arrowroot.

VEGETABLES: Beets, Swiss chard, cabbage, broccoli, white radish, kale, Napa, cucumber, winter squash, onion, garlic, string beans, broccoli, radish, cucumbers

SWEETENERS: Honey, raisins, and fruits

FRUIT & BERRIES: Apple, melon, grape, rhubarb, papaya, persimmon, boysenberry, blackberry, and strawberries.

SEASONINGS: Garlic or onion (fresh or dehydrated), basil, marjoram, cardamom, carob, fenugreek.

DAY 1 MUNCHIES
Filberts, soy nuts, walnuts, dried apples, papaya, raisins

TASTY TOPPING *Season Salt*

Sprinkle on hot or cold foods, veggies, snacks, etc.
Preheat Oven: 325°
1/2 cup sesame seeds
1/2 cup finely chopped filberts or walnuts
1 tablespoon salt (optional)
1 clove garlic, finely minced
   (Sub. 1 tsp. garlic powder)
1 Tbsp. seasoning; onion powder, basil &/or marjoram.

Mix all ingredients together, sprinkle onto large flat pan.
Bake 350° F, 10-15 minutes. Stir often. Make a double
batch and store in a glass jar in the refrigerator.

SESAME SPRINKLES *
1 cup sesame seeds
1 teaspoon salt

Try filberts or walnuts, too..

Toast seeds until light brown in 325° oven, about 10
minutes. Stir often to avoid burning; cool; grind to a fine
texture. Use in place of salt. Adds zest to boring ole'
vegetables, salads, or main dishes -- almost anything.

Hint - SALT-FREE SPRINKLES
Follow above directions, omit salt, sprinkle on waffles,
pancakes, hot or cold cereals, etc.

NUT & SEED BUTTERS, SPREADS & *MILKS*

A 'butter' can be made out of any kind of seed or nut, or combination. Day 1 - use sesame, filberts or walnuts. Use a seed/nut mill or grinder, coffee-bean grinder, blender, or a food processor (use the metal blade) to produce a fine flour, or *meal.* One cup of whole nuts or seeds yields about 1/2 cup of ground flour, or *meal.* See manufacturer's instructions.

NUT BUTTER: 1 cup meal blended with about 3 tablespoons of water or oil. Add sea salt to taste. Blend, or mix until smooth.

DIP OR SPREAD: Add liquid to butter recipe above to bring mixture to the desired consistency. Season to taste. Add chopped nuts or seeds as desired.

SAUCE OR SALAD DRESSING: Add liquid to desired consistency. Season to taste

NUT OR SEED MILK *(Designer Milks)*
1/4 cup nuts or seeds (see above) & 8 oz. water. Blend until smooth. Strain if desired. Add approximately 1 teaspoon honey **, raisin juice or fruit juice concentrate if desired. Use as a milk substitute.

** Do NOT give honey to an infant under one year of age, due to chance of botulism poisoning.

Hint - The flavor of butters, dips and spreads is improved by roasting the nuts or seeds slightly before processing. Mixing half roasted and half raw is best - you get the flavor of roasted and the nutritional value of raw.

BASIC SALAD DRESSING

1 teaspoon salt (optional)
1/8 teaspoon black pepper
1 teaspoon dry mustard
1/4 cup vinegar (sub Vit C, see p.24)
2/3 cup sesame, soy or walnut oil

Mix well, store in refrigerator. Like it? Then double or triple the recipe next time you make it.

Hint - For THICK or CREAMY dressing, add 1 tsp. guar or xanthan gum, mix well (see p22)

GREEN GODDESS DRESSING

1 sm. can anchovies - fillets or paste
3 green onions
1 clove garlic
3 cups Basic Salad Dressing *see above*

Toss in a blender, mix until smooth; or chop *really fine* & mix well. Shake before using.

MOLDED SEAFOOD SALAD

1 tablespoon unflavored gelatin
1/4 cup cold water
1/2 cup boiling water
3/4 cups basic salad dressing
1/2 cup diced onion
1 cup finely chopped cucumber
6 radishes, thinly sliced
Salt to taste
1-1/2 cups chopped or flaked cooked sea food

Soak gelatin in cold water to soften, dissolve in hot water. Mix with dressing, combine with the remaining ingredients. Pour in oiled mold and chill until firm.

MARINATED VEGGIES
Double this recipe, it's delicious and it keeps well

1/2 cup vinegar (sub Vit C, p.24)
1 or 2 cloves finely chopped garlic
1 teaspoon dried salad herbs and seasonings
1/8 cup oil (sesame, walnut or soy)
1 lb. (about 2 cups) vegetables; beets, broccoli, string
   beans, cucumber slices, onions
   May combine with frozen veggies right out of the
   package, do not cook
1 lb. cubed tofu and/or cooked beans
1/2 teaspoon salt *Optional*

In a small saucepan combine vinegar, garlic and herbs. Simmer very gently for about 5 minutes. Add oil and salt, cover and set aside to steep.

Chop vegetables into bite-sized pieces. Hard vegetables such as cauliflower, broccoli or green beans may be lightly steamed first, while others such as cucumber, or sweet onion are best if left raw. *O.K. to use frozen veggies right out of the package, do not cook.*

Bite sized pieces of raw tofu are delicious marinated, as are large cooked beans such as lima or kidney beans. Toss the vegetables into a large bowl. Some scallions or fresh herbs make a nice addition at this point. Pour marinade evenly over the vegetables and toss again. Let stand at least 1 hour, better yet - overnight - to develop full flavor. Toss from time to time to mix marinade with veggies, or marinate under pressure by placing a weighted dish on top of them inside the bowl. (A jug full of water makes a good weight).

NOTE: Marinated veggies can be added to salads, served as pickles or as a side dish. They make a nice winter salad and are a delicious accompaniment to grains, pasta and non-vegetarian main dishes. Refrigerated, most veggies keep well for 5 days, the flavor continues to develop with age.

SEASONINGS: Any fresh or dried salad herb, i.e.: basil, marjoram, oregano, mint, sage, savory, or thyme. Try adding a pinch of dulse or kelp (a dried sea vegetable).

BEAN SPROUT SALAD

1 quart (1/2 lb.) mung bean sprouts
3 green onions, cut 1/2" diagonally
4 radishes, thinly sliced
1/3 cucumber, unpeeled, thinly sliced
1/2 lb. green beans, diagonally sliced

Rinse bean sprouts. Blanch in boiling water for 3 minutes and drain in colander. Immediately dip colander into large pan of ice water to stop the cooking process. Stir gently with a fork. When cold, remove colander from water and let drain. Turn onto double thickness of paper toweling and drain thoroughly.
Mix remaining ingredients with sprouts and chill. Toss with dressing before serving.

SESAME CUCUMBER SALAD

2 cucumbers
1/2 teaspoon salt
1/2 cup dressing
1/4 cup toasted sesame seeds
2 tablespoons minced green onions

Peel cucumbers and slice very thinly. Toss everything together and chill. Serve on a bed of crisp greens.

VEGGIE-NUT BURGER - #1

1/2 cup chopped onion
1/2 cup nuts, chopped
1/4 cup flour, or an egg or egg substitute
2 tablespoons sesame or soy oil
1/2 teaspoon salt, if desired
1 clove garlic, crushed
2 cups cooked mashed squash, or beans

Combine all ingredients. Pat into shape. If dry, add
water; too moist, add arrowroot, buckwheat or nut meal
to desired consistency. Fry as patties in lightly oiled
skillet until browned nicely on both sides.

Hint - *great for a breakfast change! This is a wonderful,
versatile patty. Travels well in the car, or to school, or to
work, or traveling. Easy to mass-produce in advance.
Make up several ahead of time and freeze for future use.*

TOFUNA

Yummy as sandwich spread, topping, vegetable dip, etc.

1/2 pound tofu
1 can tuna
1/4 cup tahini (sesame butter)
1 green onion, chopped
1 small cucumber, diced
1 clove garlic, crushed (or 1 tsp. garlic powder)

Mix drained tofu and tuna, add the other stuff; mix well.

FALAFEL

Preheat Oven: 350°

2 cups cooked garbanzo beans, or 1/2 cup dry
1/2 cup cold water
1 Tbsp olive or peanut or pumpkin oil
1 clove shallots or garlic (to taste)
2 Tbsp chopped chives or leeks
1/4 tsp. pepper
1/2 tsp. each rosemary, thyme, turmeric, and/or dry
  mustard

Soak dry garbanzo beans overnight. simmer for several
hours, *see How to Cook Beans*, drain. Save liquid.
Grind, or mash until very fine (food processor works
great for this) Add liquid as needed to make a smooth
paste. Add remaining ingredients, mix well.

Hints -

BALLS:
Shape into 2 inch balls. Place on greased baking pan.
Cover with foil. Bake at 350° covered, for 15 minutes.
Turn. Bake uncovered 15 minutes. Sprinkle with chives
before serving.

SQUARES:
Easier and healthier than balls - spread 1/2" thick on
greased baking sheet. Bake covered 15 minutes,
uncovered 20 minutes; cut into 2" squares.

Great for snacks, sack lunches, travels well.

SLOW (CROCK POT) COOKING

Want to wake up to a hot breakfast? Start it at bedtime.

Hint - *Oil inside pot to prevent sticking.*

Toss into the pot:
    1 cup buckwheat or quinoa
    2 cups water
    1/2 cup raisins or cut-up, dried apple, papaya or
    berries
    Pinch of salt, if desired

Turn on low before retiring. In the morning, sweeten with honey(if desired), add nut milk and enjoy. After breakfast, stuff the leftover cereal in zip-lock bag, flatten, seal, label, toss in the freezer -- and then start dinner:

Rinse out the pot, add a pot roast or stewing (or roasting) hen, toss in some onions, string beans and/or squash. Dinner will be ready when you are. Corned beef and cabbage are great prepared in this method.

To cook meat or poultry overnight: Place in pot before bedtime without vegetables. Have a bit of the meat for breakfast if you like, or pack a little in your lunch bag. Then place the vegetables in the pot, on top of what's left of the meat, and let simmer until lunch or dinner time.

Old Fashioned Bean Soups and stews are a welcome treat any time of the day or night. Cook up a huge batch, freeze for more hurried or hectic times.

GREAT GARLIC SOUP *Wonderful for colds and flu*

1 large head of fresh garlic
1 quart water
2 whole cloves
2 quarts chicken broth
3 cups kidney beans , or soy or lima as desired)
Handful of stuffed green olives, sliced (optional)
Season to taste: onion, basil &/or marjoram

Separate the cloves of garlic and peel by layering on a cutting board and slapping hard with the flat side of a large bladed knife. The skin will fall away. Combine all ingredients, simmer at least one hour. Pour into a blender, blend until smooth (puree), reheat and serve garnished with green olives.

ONION SOUP   *Excellent by itself or as stock.*

1 tablespoon oil or butter
3 cups chopped onion
2 tablespoons flour (buckwheat, quinoa, soy or arrowroot)
6 cups water
1 tsp. basil or marjoram.   Salt and pepper to taste

Sauté onion in oil/butter until brown. Blend in flour, gradually stir in water. Add salt and pepper if desired, and cook over low heat for 30 minutes. Serve hot. For a main dish, add chunks of cooked seafood or shell fish and heat thoroughly.

SEAFOOD BOUILLON
Delicious Basic Stock

2 lbs. fish trimmings or 1/2 lb. of fresh fish pieces
2 quarts water
1 tsp. seasoning: garlic or onion, basil, marjoram,
   cardamom, fenugreek.
1 pat of butter or 1 tsp. oil
1 large onion, sliced   2 teaspoons salt

Sauté onion in butter/oil until golden brown. Add
remaining ingredients and simmer for 1 hour; strain. It
can be made ahead and kept in a covered jar in the
refrigerator, or frozen for several weeks.

CHICKEN VEGETABLE SOUP

1 stewing hen, (fryer is OK)
1 chopped onion
1 lb. cut-up string beans
1 bunch Swiss chard, chopped
2 cups squash, cut into 2" squares
2 teaspoons salt (opt)
1/4 teaspoon pepper
2-1/2 quarts water

Rinse chicken and place in a 6-quart kettle. Add 2 cups
water and simmer 2 hours, or until tender. Sauté onion
until brown. Add with remaining ingredients, bring to
boil, reduce heat and simmer at least 1 hour.

CURRIED LENTILS

4 cups cooked lentils
1 large sliced onion
1 clove garlic, chopped; or 1 tsp. garlic powder
1 cup cut-up string beans
1 tsp. sesame, soy or walnut oil
2 tablespoons mild curry powder (more or less to taste)
1-1/2 cups water or vegetable broth

Sauté onion in oil. Stir in curry powder. Gradually add water or broth. Combine all ingredients, mix well. Simmer until string beans are tender. Serve hot.

COMPANY CAULIFLOWER

1 medium size head cauliflower
1 teaspoon tarragon leaves, crumbled
1/2 teaspoon salt
1/16 teaspoon ground white pepper
1/2 teaspoon paprika

Wash cauliflower thoroughly; remove outer leaves and core, keeping head intact. Place in 1" boiling water in a large saucepan or skillet. Add tarragon and white pepper. Add cauliflower and cook for 10 minutes basting frequently with tarragon flavored liquid. Cover, reduce heat and simmer 15 to 20 minutes longer or until tender. Carefully remove cauliflower to serving dish. Dust with paprika.

NUTTY STUFFED ONIONS

Serves six

3/4 cup chopped filberts, walnuts, or sesame seeds
6 large onions (3 lbs.)
1 teaspoon salt
1 cucumber, diced
1/4 cup fresh mint, chopped
1/2 cup sesame, walnut or soy oil
1/4 cup vinegar or Vit C (see p. 24)
1/4 teaspoon pepper
Cabbage leaves or Swiss chard or
   radishes for garnish

Optional: May add 1 cup cooked buckwheat groats or beans to mixture, if desired.
Steam onions until tender. Cut 1 inch off tops, pull out middle, (save) leaving a firm shell. Invert on paper toweling for 30 minutes to drain.

Chop onion middles, toss gently with cucumber, mint, oil, vinegar, nuts, spice, salt and pepper.

To assemble - spoon nut mixture into shells, mounding slightly. Arrange on platter lined with cabbage or Swiss chard leaves.

Top with additional nuts and sprigs of fresh mint.

FRESH FISH WITH A K.I.S.S.

(Keep it Simple, Sweetie)   Serves 6 to 8

3 tablespoons sesame oil or butter
3 tablespoons chopped walnuts or filberts
2 lbs. fish fillets (see p.p.)
1 tablespoon apple juice or vinegar (see p. 24)
1/2 teaspoon garlic powder
1/4 teaspoon pepper

Heat 2 tablespoons of oil in a large skillet. Add nuts and sauté over a medium heat 2 to 3 minutes until golden brown, stirring constantly. Remove nuts and set aside. In remaining oil, cook fish 3 to 4 minutes on each side until done. Remove to a warm platter and season with salt and pepper. Stir remaining ingredients into pan drippings; add nuts, stir again and spoon over fish.

Even more simple;
Sprinkle fish with tasty topping (see p.35), sauté until tender.

Like it crispy?
Sprinkle with tasty topping; coat with ground sesame seeds, walnuts or filberts, bake or fry until golden brown.

Healthy Fish with a K.I.S.S. , con't:

Baked fillets: Rinse fish, place in greased baking dish. Sprinkle with tasty topping or above seasonings, bake in preheated hot oven (400 F) about 20 minutes.

Serve with coleslaw, pickled beets, and/or steamed vegetables and baked squash.

CHICKEN AND BROCCOLI BAKE

Preheat Oven: 375°

2 -10 oz. packages frozen broccoli*
4 tablespoons arrowroot (thickener)
2 cups chicken broth
1 lb. cooked chicken, sliced*
1/2 cup chopped walnuts, filberts, or sesame seeds

Mix thickener and chicken broth in a shaker, so that it does not lump. Cook over a medium heat until thickened and smooth. Season to taste. Place broccoli pieces in a baking dish and cover with chicken. Pour gravy mixture over the chicken and broccoli. Sprinkle with chopped nuts. Bake uncovered 20 to 25 minutes until bubbly and browned.

*Preferred method: Use uncooked chicken pieces and **fresh** broccoli, increase cooking time to 1 hour.

Hint -Turkey or rabbit may be substituted for chicken.

CURRIED CHICKEN

Serves 6 to 8

1 cut-up chicken (or 1 1/2# chicken parts)
1 teaspoon salt
1/2 teaspoon pepper
1 tablespoon sesame or soy or walnut oil
3/4 teaspoon curry powder
1/4 teaspoon powdered ginger
1-1/2 cups water
3 chicken bouillon cubes, crumbled
1-1/2 tablespoons arrowroot
1 tablespoon apple juice
1 tsp. ascorbic acid powder (Vit. C)

Season thighs with salt and pepper. In a heavy skillet, brown chicken slowly on all sides using just enough oil to prevent sticking. Add curry powder and ginger and sauté slowly for 5 minutes. Stir in water and bouillon cubes. Cover and simmer 1 hour or until chicken is tender. Remove chicken and keep warm. Skim off and discard any fat from juices.

Blend arrowroot with 2 tablespoons of cold water. Stir into liquid remaining in pan. Cook, stirring until sauce boils and thickens slightly. Stir in the apple juice. Serve chicken with thickened pan juices on the side, or served on buckwheat groats or bean noodles.

SAVORY BROILED CHICKEN

Great dish for company

1/4 cup vinegar *
1 teaspoon crushed garlic
1 teaspoon sesame, soy or walnut oil
1/2 teaspoon salt
1/2 teaspoon ground ginger
1/2 teaspoon paprika
1/4 teaspoon instant onion powder
1/4 teaspoon ground black pepper
2-1/2 lbs. broiler-fryer chicken, quartered

*Sub 1 Tbsp. Vit. C crystals in 1/4 cup water (see p.24)

In a small bowl, combine vinegar, garlic, oil, ginger, paprika, onion powder and pepper; mix well. Brush over chicken. Place chicken in broiler pan, skin side down. Broil 7 to 9 inches from heat source for 10 minutes. Turn chicken, turn and bast occasionally, until browned and crisp, about 25 minutes longer.

MEALS WITH A K.I.S.S.
(Keep It Simple, Sweetie)

Steam a fresh vegetable*; or place frozen vegetables in small saucepan, cover and heat slowly; then microwave a piece of squash while steaming or sauteing a fish fillet. Sprinkle with *Tasty Topping* - enjoy.

* beets, swiss chard, cabbage, broccoli, kale, Napa, squash, onions, string beans.

OLD FASHIONED POT ROAST Yield: 10 portions

3-1/2 lbs. lean brisket of beef
1 large chopped onion
1 small bay leaf
1/2 teaspoon salt
1/2 teaspoon black pepper, coarsely ground
1/4 teaspoon garlic, minced

Brown meat for 10 minutes on each side in a dutch oven or heavy saucepan. Add 1 cup water and remaining ingredients. Cover and cook very slowly 3 to 4 hours or until tender. Pour juices in a small bowl (keep roast hot, or re-heat before serving) and chill until fat forms a hard layer on the top; remove fat and discard. Heat juices, thicken with arrowroot, if desired.

Hint - Add vegetables of the day on top of roast about 1 hour before serving, cook until tender. *See crock pot cookery*

PONSET   *Delightful noodle dish*

1/2 lb. noodles (mung bean or buckwheat)*
1 chopped onion
2 cloves garlic, pressed
2 cups chopped cabbage, broccoli, or Napa
1 cup cooked, cubed chicken or seafood
1 tsp. soy sauce, or salt (if desired) and/or toasted sesame oil

Hint - *Sprouts or cooked whole grain may be substituted for noodles

Ponset, con't --

Soak noodles in very hot water; drain. Sauté onion and garlic in oil or small amount of water, add remaining vegetables, sauté until tender. Season to taste. Toss together with remaining ingredients, serve hot.

Optional: *Sprinkle with toasted sesame seeds*

KOREAN BROILED STEAK (Kun Koki)

1 flank steak or chuck steak (2 lbs.)
3 tablespoons sesame seeds
1 tablespoon sesame oil
1 tablespoon soy sauce or 1/2 teaspoon salt
2 cloves garlic, crushed
1/2 teaspoon black pepper
1/2 teaspoon ginger
1/8 cup vinegar or dry wine
1/4 cup apple juice
2 green onions, sliced

Score steak and place in glass dish. Combine other ingredients and marinate several hours or overnight. Broil steak about 5 minutes per side or as you like it.

Hint - This is an easy, impressive, do-ahead dinner idea for company. Serve with Savory string beans and salad. Marinade works great for fish, poultry or tofu, too.

CRACKERS & PIE CRUSTS

Made From Flour:
2 cups buckwheat, arrowroot, squash or bean flour
1 teaspoon baking powder or soda
1 teaspoon salt
1/3 cup sesame, soy or walnut oil or butter
1/3 cup cold water (approximate measure)

Combine flour, baking powder or soda and salt, mix
well, add oil or fat and mix with a fork until crumbly.
Add water slowly, as needed, form into 2 balls.
Chill thoroughly.

Made From Nuts Or Seeds:
2 cups nut or seed meal: sesame, filbert, or walnut.
1 tsp. baking powder
1 tsp. salt (opt)
1/3 cup thickener (arrowroot or bean flour)

Combine flour, baking powder or soda and salt. Mix
well, add oil or fat and mix with a fork until crumbly.
Add water slowly, as needed, form into 2 balls.
Chill thoroughly.

PIE CRUST

Roll chilled ball out and place into pie pan*, or place ball
in pan and press into place, flute edge as desired. Prick
with fork. Bake at 350° for approximately 15 minutes,
cool and add filling. Chill before serving.

See next page ->

Hint - Instead of trying to roll out the bottom crust, place the ball of dough in a greased (sprayed is even better) pie pan or dish; pat it flat with your fingers - then gently coax the dough into a 1/8" thick crust. Even-out the lumps with a flat-bottomed glass.

Hint - Oil is not usually needed with nuts and seeds. But if the crust is too tough, add oil the next time.

CRACKERS   Preheat Oven: 350°

Place ball of chilled dough on lightly greased baking sheet, roll out to about 1/4" thick. Dust dough lightly with flour as necessary to keep from sticking to rolling pin. Cut into 2" squares. Prick with fork all over. Bake in middle of preheated oven 350° for 10 minutes or until brown. (Time varies depending on type of flour used.) Watch carefully to prevent burning.

Hint - If dough is too sticky, don't panic! Just gently stretch and pat into place with floured fingers. *Next time use less liquid.*

Options: Add 1/2 teaspoon seasoning, choose from: basil, marjoram, cardamom, garlic powder.
Sprinkle with chopped walnuts, filberts or sesame seeds and roll again or pat gently, before baking.
Cut into fun shapes with cookie cutters - make diamonds, stripes, hearts, circles or whatever.

Hint - Save broken and odd-shapes, crumble and use like cracker or bread crumbs, for croutons, stuffings, etc.

BASIC MUFFINS

Preheat Oven: 350°

Yield: 12 lg. or 18 small muffins

1-1/2 cups flour (buckwheat or soy) or
  meal (filbert, sesame or walnut)
1/2 cup arrowroot
1 teaspoon baking powder
1/2 teaspoon salt (optional)
1 egg or substitute (see p.23)
1/3 cup sesame, soy or walnut oil
1 cup liquid: (sesame, soy, filbert or walnut milk)
  or juice: (apple, papaya, grape or berry)

Sift dry ingredients, mix together. Combine wet ingredients, mix well. Add wet mixture to dry, stirring until just blended; do not over beat. Fill greased muffin cups 1/2 full. Bake 12 to 15 minutes.

Variations: add chopped nuts &/or chopped, dried papaya.

Apple spice: add 1 cup chopped apple, or 1/2 cup apple sauce (reduce liquid to 1/2 cup); 1/2 cup finely chopped walnuts or filberts, 1/2 cup raisins, 2 teaspoons cinnamon and 1/2 teaspoon nutmeg.

Hint - Instead of mixing nuts & fruit with batter, place on top of uncooked muffin and they won't sink to the bottom.

Recipe adapted from *Super Grains*, Marge Jones

NUTRI OLA   Tasty - Allergy-free Granola

Versatile: Cereal -- Breakfast Bar -- Snack Bar
        Yield: 10 portions   Preheat Oven 275°

2 cups arrowroot, buckwheat flour or finely ground
  filberts, walnuts or sesame seeds.
1 cup filberts or walnuts, coarsely ground
1 cup whole sesame seeds
1 cup finely chopped, dried apples, papaya or raisins
1/2 cup honey or concentrated frozen fruit juice or fruit
  puree
1/4 cup sesame, walnut or soy oil
2 teaspoons vanilla

Use a blender and or food processor to grind nuts,
grains or seeds to desired consistency. Mix the nuts,
seeds and/or grains in a large bowl. Mix together fruit,
sweetener, oil and vanilla. Pour over the dry mixture and
stir lightly. Spread mixture into a lightly oiled baking pan
(15 x 10 x 1"). Bake for 1 hour stirring every 15 minutes.
Cool. Break into small pieces for cereal or large chunks
for snacks. Store in air tight, labeled container.

Nutri Ola Snack Bars
Add to basic recipe --
2 eggs (or egg substitute), slowly add additional liquid
(water or juice) to make a stiff batter. Follow above
directions, bake at 325 F about 30 minutes, cut into
squares when done.

Hint - Taste batter before baking and make sure you
like it. Add more sweetener or salt if desired.

BASIC PANCAKES - Made with Flour

1-1/2 cups buckwheat, arrowroot or soy flour
1/4 teaspoon salt
1 tablespoon baking powder
1 egg (or substitute, see p. 24)
1-3/4 cups liquid: sesame, filbert, walnut, or soy milk; or
  apple, papaya, grape or berry juice.
1/8 cup sesame, walnut or soy oil
1 tablespoon honey (optional)

Combine dry ingredients and mix well. Combine egg, liquid, oil and honey, then add to dry ingredients. Bake on preheated, non- stick griddle, turn when browned and bubbly. Cool on wire rack so they don't stick together.

Hint - If batter thickens (it usually does), add small amounts of liquid as needed.

Hint - For an even lighter 'cake', omit soda and mix the night before, then add soda just before cooking. Bean and other heavy flours yield a finer finished product the longer they 'soak'; freezing further improves texture.

Double the recipe and use extras like slices of bread.

Build multi-layered sandwiches, or spread with fillings and roll them up jelly roll fashion (like crepes or burritos). Great for Lunches: use your imagination for fillings, anything goes. (See lunch suggestions).

BASIC PANCAKES - Made with Nuts or Seeds

2 cups filbert or sesame meal (see p.27)
1 teaspoon baking powder or soda
1 teaspoon salt (optional)   ·
1/3 cup arrowroot
1/3 cup liquid: sesame, filbert, walnut or soy milk; or
   apple, papaya, grape or berry juice.
1 egg or substitute (see p.23)

Combine dry ingredients and mix well. Combine egg,
liquid, oil and honey, then add to dry ingredients. Bake
on preheated, non- stick griddle, turn when browned
and bubbly.

Hint - If batter thickens (it usually does), add small
amounts of liquid as needed. Oil is not needed when
nuts or seeds are used instead of a flour. Add ground or
chopped nuts or seeds for variety.

Hint - **Double the recipe** and use extras like slices
of bread. Cool on wire rack so they don't stick together.

Build multi-layered sandwiches, or spread with
fillings and roll them up jelly roll fashion (like crepes or
burritos).

Great for lunches and travel: use your imagination
for fillings, anything goes. (See lunch suggestions).
Store in refrigerator &/or package as individual servings.

BEANCAKE PANCAKES

1/2 cup soy or lima bean flour
1/4 cup arrowroot flour
1 egg or egg substitute (see p.23)
3/4 cup water
1/4 teaspoon salt (optional)
1/2 teaspoon soda
1/2 cup finely chopped nuts (optional)

Mix together egg substitute and water, let stand about 10 minutes. Combine bean flour, salt, soda and chopped nuts. Mix well with wet ingredients and let stand about 10 minutes until mixture thickens. Bake on preheated, non- stick griddle, turn when browned and bubbly.

Place on a warm platter, and sprinkle with cheese (if allowed) or any other topping; place in a warm oven until cheese melts.

Hint - Double or even triple this recipe, cool on wire rack, or place towels in between until cool so they won't stick together. Add ground or chopped nuts or seeds for variety. Store in refrigerator & use as sandwich material. Package as individual servings and freeze for lunches and travel.

Build multi-layered sandwiches, or spread with fillings and roll them up jelly roll fashion (like crepes or burritos). Great for lunches: use your imagination for fillings, anything goes. (See lunch suggestions).

Thanks to Pauline Adams

BASIC WAFFLES - made with flour

1-1/2 cups flour (buckwheat, arrowroot or soy)
1/4 teaspoon salt
1 tablespoon baking powder
1 egg (or substitute, see p. 23)
1-3/4 cups liquid: sesame, filbert, walnut, soy milk;
     or apple, papaya, grape or berry juice.
1/8 cup sesame, soy or walnut oil
1 tablespoon honey (optional)

Combine dry ingredients , mix well. Combine egg, liquid,
oil and honey together, mix and add to dry ingredients.
Bake in **pre-heated** waffle iron, *with a non-stick
surface. This is important! Heavy flours tend to stick*
Otherwise, you'll be scraping off the waffle in bits and
pieces & cursing me --- not a good way to start the day.

BASIC WAFFLES made with Nuts or Seeds

2 cups filbert or sesame meal (see p.27)
1 teaspoon baking powder or soda
1 teaspoon salt, (optional)
1/3 cup flour or thickener
1/3 cup liquid: sesame, filbert, walnut, soy milk; or apple,
     papaya, grape or berry juice.
1/8 cup sesame, soy or walnut oil
I egg (or substitute, see p. 23)

Use the same mixing and baking instructions as above.

HEAVENLY NUT BREAD

Moist and wonderful!   *Pre-heat oven 350°F.*

2 cups flour (buckwheat or soy) - or -
   1&1/2 cups meal (filbert, sesame or walnut)
   plus 1/2 cup arrowroot
1-1/2 teaspoons baking soda
1/2 teaspoon salt, if desired
1 teaspoon ground cardamom
1 teaspoon allspice
1/2 teaspoon cloves
1 cup raisins
1 cup chopped filberts or walnuts
1-1/2 cups fruit puree or honey
1 cup apple or papaya juice
3 eggs or substitute
1-1/2 cups winter squash (cooked and pureed)
1-1/2 teaspoons vanilla

Combine dry ingredients together and mix well.
Combine wet ingredients together and mix well.
Gradually and gently blend wet and dry ingredients
together. Batter will be very thick. Spread in sprayed or
oiled and floured pans and bake at 325° for about 1
hour until a knife or toothpick inserted in the middle
comes out clean.

Hint - Two small loaf pans work better than a large
one. Less chance of ending up with a *soggy middle.*
Lord knows, we don't want any of those.
This nut loaf keeps well refrigerated - if it lasts that long.

NUT BUTTER COOKIES

Simple and tasty, too!

Preheat Oven: 350°   Yield: 2-1/2 doz.

1 cup nut butter (sesame, walnut or filbert, see p.27)
1/2 cup honey
1/2 teaspoon vanilla
1/4 teaspoon salt (optional)
2 cups flour (buckwheat or soy or arrow root)
  or meal: (filbert, sesame or walnut)

Preheat oven to 350°. Mix nut butter, sweetener and oil together until smooth. Add flavoring and salt and blend again. Add flour or starch a little at a time and mix well.

Use a wooden spoon, or better yet, mix with your hands; **do not use an electric mixer**!

Roll dough into balls, place on oiled cookie sheet, flatten with a fork. **Or** form into 2" thick rolls on waxed paper. Roll up, chill and   slice 1/2" thick.

Bake about 12 minutes, **watch closely** to avoid burning.
Uncooked dough keeps well in refrigerator. Bake as needed. Freezes nicely also.

SUGAR-FREE SWEET TREATS
The following two "uncandies" are great for lunches or snacks any time of the day and are great travelers.

APPLE - WALNUT BARS

2 cups dried fruit: raisins, papaya or apples
2 cups walnuts, filberts or sesame seeds
Pinch of salt, optional
1/2 teaspoon flavoring, if desired

Food Processor: Cut fruit into small pieces, toss into the food processor; add nuts or seeds, blend until ball forms. Use the metal chopping blade.
Blender: Cut up fruit, place in blender and chop fine. Chop nuts separately, mix with fruit. Use sturdy spoon to mix and knead, or use fingers. If too dry to mix well, a small amount of water or juice. Batter will Be *very* stiff
Press firmly into oiled pie pan or cookie sheet, cut in squares; or place on waxed paper; form into 2" roll - or in little balls - roll in additional chopped nuts or seeds; . Wrap logs in waxed paper or foil (shiny side next to food). chill and slice as needed. Store in refrigerator.

NUT BUTTER *CANDY*

1 cup nut butter
1/4 cup carob powder
1/4 cup honey, or to taste
1/2 cup chopped nuts (filbert or walnut)
    or toasted sesame seeds

Toss into food processor, mix well; or use sturdy spoon to mix. Then follow the above mixing directions -- starting with **Press** *firmly--*

Day 2

Yellow Day

FOOD CHOICES FOR DAY 2

Day 2 and Day 4 foods and recipes are interchangeable. You may switch them back and forth, just remember to wait for four days before eating that food again.

Proteins
Fish may be eaten daily as long as a different fish is selected each day; shrimp, lobster. Turkey & turkey eggs.

Nuts, seeds & oils
Almonds, almond oil, apricot oil, pine & brazil nuts, sunflower seeds & oil.

Grains, flours, misc.
Millet, rice, rye, spelt, potato flour, flax seed meal, xanthan gum.

Vegetables
Carrots, parsley, leaf & bib lettuce, common artichoke, white potato, peppers, yams, jicama, mushrooms.

Fruits
Plum, prune, apricot, lemon, orange, kumquat, huckleberries, cranberries, kiwi, guava.

Sweeteners
Dates, molasses, rice syrup, fruits, concentrated fruit juices..

Seasonings
Chili, bell peppers, fennel, celery seed & leaves, cilantro, cumin.

TASTY TOPPING *Season Salt* *Preheat Oven: 375°*

Sprinkle on hot or cold foods, veggies, snacks, etc.

1 cup chopped almonds, brazil or pine nuts, or
    sunflower seeds
1 tablespoon salt (optional)
1 Tbsp. seasonings - choose from:
    caraway, chervil, dill seed & dill weed, parsley, or
    dash of cayenne.

Mix all ingredients together, sprinkle onto large flat pan.
Bake 350° F, 10-15 minutes. Stir often. Make a double
batch and store in a glass jar in the refrigerator.

ALMOND SPRINKLES * *Preheat Oven: 325°*

1 cup ground, roasted almonds
1 teaspoon salt
* *Try brazil nuts or sunflower seeds, too.*

Toast nuts or seeds until light brown in 325° oven, about
10 minutes. Stir to avoid burning. Place in blender, grind
to a fine texture. Use in place of salt. Adds zest to boring
ole' vegetables, salads, or main dishes -- almost
anything.

Hint - **SALT-FREE SPRINKLES**
Follow above directions, omit salt, sprinkle on waffles,
pancakes, hot or cold cereals, etc.

NUT & SEED BUTTERS, SPREADS & MILKS

A 'butter' can be made out of any kind of seed or nut, or combination. Day 2: Almonds, pine & brazil nuts, sunflower seeds.
Use a seed/nut mill or grinder, coffee-bean grinder, blender, or a food processor (use the metal blade) to produce a fine flour, or *meal.* One cup of whole nuts or seeds yields about 1/2 cup of ground flour, or *meal.* See manufacturer's instructions.

NUT BUTTER: 1 cup meal blended with about 3 tablespoons of water or oil. Add sea salt to taste. Blend, or mix until smooth.

DIP OR SPREAD: Add liquid to butter recipe above to bring mixture to the desired consistency. Season to taste. Add chopped nuts or seeds as desired.

SAUCE OR SALAD DRESSING: Add liquid to desired consistency. Season to taste

NUT OR SEED MILK *(Designer Milks)*
1/4 cup nuts or seeds (see above) & 8 oz. water.
Blend until smooth. Strain if desired. Add approximately 1 teaspoon honey **, raisin juice or fruit juice concentrate if desired. Use as a milk substitute.

*** Do NOT give honey to an infant under one year of age, due to chance of botulism poisoning.*

Hint: The flavor of butters, dips and spreads is improved by roasting the nuts or seeds slightly before grinding them. Half raw and half roasted is best - retains more nutritional value.

BASIC SALAD DRESSING

1 teaspoon salt (optional)
1/8 teaspoon cayenne pepper
1 teaspoon dill weed or dried parsley
 Dash of Tabasco
1/4 cup lemon juice
2/3 cup sunflower, almond, or apricot oil

Mix well, store in refrigerator. Double - or even triple - the recipe for convenience.

Hint - For *THICK or CREAMY* dressing, add 1 tsp. guar or xanthan gum, mix well (see p.22)

GREEN GODDESS DRESSING

1 sm. can anchovies
handful of parsley
8 - 10 leaves fresh tarragon, or
    2 teaspoons dried
3 cups **Basic Salad Dressing**

Blend in a blender until smooth, or chop fine & mix well. Shake well, enjoy.

GALA SALAD

1 head leaf or bib lettuce
6 carrots, chopped
4 celery stalks, chopped
1 jicama, peeled and chopped
3 jalapeno chilies, sliced
Fresh sprouts

Separate lettuce leaves and place on a platter. Mound remaining ingredients on top of the lettuce, alternating colors. Serve with salad dressing (see p.70).

JICAMA

Jicama (hee'kah'mah): A crispy, yet juicy vegetable. Does not darken when cut. Lovingly called the "poor person's water chestnut" because it stays crisp when heated.

Serve it raw, in salads or with dips. Add to soups, stir-fry or stews. *My favorite* is equal parts of grated jicama and carrots sprinkled with lime juice or liquid Vit. C (p24).

In it's native Mexico it is served on large platters with slices of orange for color. Sprinkle with lime or lemon and chili powder. Garnish with parsley.

Usually available November to June. Store in a cool dry place. *Scrub with soap and water before peeling.* Refrigerate after peeling.

CURRIED SHRIMP OR TUNA SALAD

It's deee-licious with or without curry
1 cup cooked shrimp
2 cups brown rice, cooked *
1 medium green pepper, shredded
1 cup chopped celery
1 cup sliced raw mushrooms
2 tablespoons pimiento, chopped
2 tablespoons parsley, chopped
1/8 cup sunflower, almond or apricot oil
1/3 cup lemon juice
1/2 teaspoon curry
Dash of cayenne if desired.

*Rice is optional - you may substitute any grain, or sprouts or chopped nuts or seeds.

Mix shrimp or tuna, rice, celery, green pepper, mushrooms, pimiento and parsley together. Combine oil, lemon juice and curry. Toss together. Chill several hours before serving.
Make a day ahead of time, flavor improves with time.

MARINATED SEAFOOD SALAD

1 lb. firm fish (canned fish is OK)
1/4 cup *basic salad dressing*
Small bunch of parsley, finely chopped
1 bell pepper, finely chopped
5 sliced raw mushrooms (optional)
1/4 cup grated jicama, if desired

Salad, Con't ...

2 grated carrots
1 teaspoon seasoning, choose from:
    anise, caraway, chervil, dill seed or weed, parsley,
    pimento, &/or *dash* of cayenne.
1/3 cup sunflower or almond oil
Salt to taste

Poach, drain and chill fish. See instructions, p.170) Cut
fish into bite-sized cubes and marinate with the other
ingredients at least 1 hour before serving.

MOLDED SEAFOOD SALAD

1 tablespoon unflavored gelatin
1/4 cup cold water
1/2 cup boiling water
3/4 cups salad dressing
1/2 cup grated carrots
10 green olives, chopped
1/2 green pepper, minced
1/2 cup minced parsley
1 teaspoon cilantro
1/2 teaspoon salt
1-1/2 cups cooked seafood, chopped or flaked
2 tablespoons pimentos, chopped

Soak gelatin in cold water to soften, dissolve in hot
water. Mix with dressing, combine with the remaining
ingredients, pour in oiled mold and chill until firm. Serve
on fresh greens.

MARINATED VEGGIES

(Double this recipe, it keeps well)

1/3 cup lemon juice
1 teaspoon dried salad herbs and seasonings
  (paprika, pimento, caraway, celery seed,
  chervil, cumin, dill, fennel, &/or parsley)
1/8 cup oil (sunflower, almond, or apricot)
1 lb. (about 2 cups) of Day 2 vegetables
  *May use frozen veggies right out of the
  package, do not cook*
1/2 teaspoon salt *Optional*

In a small saucepan combine vinegar, garlic and herbs.
Simmer very gently for about 5 minutes. Add oil and salt,
cover and set aside to steep.

Cut vegetables into bite- sized pieces. Hard vegetables
such as carrots, jicama, artichokes may be lightly
steamed first, while others such as parsley, mushrooms,
sweet peppers are best if left raw. Toss vegetables, etc.
with salt in a large bowl. Fresh herbs make a nice
addition at this point. Pour marinade evenly over the
vegetables and toss again. Let sit at least 1 hour, best
overnight, to develop full flavor. Toss from time to time to
mix marinade with veggies, or marinate under pressure
by placing a weighted dish on top of them inside the
bowl. (A jug full of water makes a good weight).

Marinated veggies, con't --

Note: Marinated veggies can be mixed into salads, served as pickles or as a side dish. They make a nice winter salad and are a delicious accompaniment to grains, pasta and non-vegetarian main dishes. Refrigerated, they will keep will for 5 days, the flavor continues to develop with time.

NUTTY STUFFED PEPPERS
Great as a main course or a side dish

1 cup chopped almonds, brazil or
   whole pine nuts or sunflower seeds
6 large bell peppers
Salt to taste
1 cup fresh parsley, chopped
1/2 cup celery, diced
1 tsp. anise, dill or caraway seed
1/4 cup lemon juice
1/4 teaspoon pepper
lettuce leaves   lemon wedges
Optional: Add 1 cup cooked brown or wild rice or
   millet to stuffing mixture.

Slice top off peppers, (about 1"). Scoop out seeds, add to fresh veggies. Steam peppers until tender. Invert on paper toweling for 30 minutes to drain. Mix together all remaining ingredients, except lettuce and lemon wedges, toss gently. Stuff into the peppers, mounding slightly. Top each with additional nuts. Arrange on lettuce lined salad platter. Garnish with lemon wedges. Chill before serving.

TERRIFIC TURKEY SALAD

1/8 cup sunflower or almond oil
1/3 cup lemon juice
1 sprig parsley, minced
1 teaspoon tarragon
1 teaspoon dill weed
1/4 teaspoon salt
1/8 teaspoon paprika
1 cup cubed turkey or shrimp
2 cups cooked rice or millet , or
    substitute chopped, cooked carrots or potatoes;
    or sliced raw jicama or mushrooms

Toss vegetables (or rice or millet) together with remaining ingredients. Toss gently. Cover and chill several hours. Serve on bed of lettuce. Sprinkle with chopped almonds, pine or brazil nuts, or sunflower seeds.

ALMOND VEGETABLES

4 cups frozen (thawed) or steamed vegetables
    Choice of: carrots, parsley, artichokes, potatoes,
    bell peppers, yams, jicama, mushrooms.
1/8 cup almond or sunflower oil
1/4 cup chopped or slivered almonds or sunflower seeds
Almond salt to taste (or sea salt)

Cook vegetables until tender but crisp. Drain. Heat oil in skillet. Add almonds or seeds and stir until sizzling. Add vegetables and gently heat through. Season to taste.

ALMOND SOUP

2 cups blanched almonds
4 cups water
3 tablespoons almond or sunflower oil
1/2 cup fresh (1 small can) sliced mushrooms
Grated peel of 1 or 2 lemons
Seeds from 2 - 3 cardamom pods
Salt, to taste

Combine all ingredients in a blender. Blend until smooth, pour mixture into a medium sized saucepan. Cover and simmer gently for 1 hour.

PEASANT VEGETABLE SOUP

1 bell pepper, chopped
1/4 lb. mushrooms, chopped
3 large carrots, thinly sliced
1 sprig parsley, chopped
1 cup each cubed potatoes, yams, and/or jicama
1 tablespoon sunflower or almond oil
8 cups water
1 Tbsp. seasonings - oregano, caraway, chervil,
dill seed &/or parsley. Salt to taste

Sauté peppers and mushrooms in oil. Add the water and remaining ingredients in a large pot, bring to boil, the simmer covered over low heat for at least one hour, flavor improves with age. (See crock pot/slow cookery p.164).

SEAFOOD BOUILLON (Basic Stock)

2 lbs. fish trimmings (see p.168-170)
2 quarts water
1 cup chopped bell peppers
1/8 cup oil
2 carrots, sliced
3 sprigs parsley   Salt to taste
1 tsp. seasoning: anise, caraway, chervil,
   dill weed, parsley.

Sauté vegetables in oil, combine remaining ingredients
and simmer for 1 hour; strain. Pour into container, cover.
Refrigerate up to three days or freeze indefinitely.

TURKEY VEGETABLE SOUP

1 large turkey hindquarter (about 3#)
3 medium carrots, sliced
2 stalks celery with tops, sliced
1/4 teaspoon pepper   Salt to taste
1/2 teaspoon dried basil leaves
2-1/2 quarts water
1 cup mushrooms, chopped
1/4 cup (rice, millet or rye) flour, or 2 diced potatoes
1/2 cup fresh parsley, chopped, for garnish.

Rinse turkey and place in a 6-quart kettle. Bring to boil.
Reduce heat and simmer until tender (2 - 3 hours). Sauté
onion in 1 teaspoon oil until brown, add to kettle along
with the remaining ingredients, simmer at least another
1/2 hour.

SLOW (CROCK POT) COOKING

Breakfast can be simple if you start it at bedtime. (See `cooking whole grains').

Oil inside of the pot to prevent sticking.
Add:
    1/2 cup rice, millet, or rye
    2 cups water
    1/2 cup cut-up, dried prunes or apricots.
    Pinch of salt, if desired
Turn on low before retiring.

In the morning, sweeten with molasses or rice syrup if desired, add nut milk and enjoy.

Empty the pot after breakfast and start dinner:
Place a turkey half, hindquarter or wings in the pot, add 2 cups of water and cut-up carrots, potatoes, yams &/or jicama.
Dinner will be ready by 5 p.m.

Can't have grain?
Follow the procedure for cooking turkey:
place in pot before bedtime without vegetables. Have the turkey for breakfast & pack some to take in your lunch .
Then place the vegetables in the pot, on top of the meat, and let cook until lunch or dinner time.

Old Fashioned turkey soup (see recipe), is a welcome and nourishing treat any time of day or night.

VEGGIE BURGER Dujour #2

Great recipe. Make in advance, keeps well

1/2 cup celery, chopped
1 sprig chopped parsley
1/2 cup chopped almonds, pine or brazil nuts,
    or sunflower seeds
1/4 cup potato flour or egg or egg substitute
2 tablespoons sunflower, almond, or apricot oil
1/2 teaspoon salt if desired
2 cups cooked grated or mashed potatoes, yams or
jicama

Combine all ingredients. Pat into shape. If dry, add water; too moist, add potato flour or flax seed meal or nut meal to desired consistency. Fry as patties in lightly oiled skillet until browned nicely on both sides.

Hint: Great for a breakfast change!

Hint: This is a wonderful, versatile patty. Travels well, easy to pack and take in the car, or to school, or to work, or traveling.

Hint: Easy to mass-produce in advance. Make up several ahead of time and freeze for future use.

FISH WITH A K.I.S.S *Keep it Simple, Sweetie*

Yield: 6 portions

1 Tbsp sunflower or almond oil
3 tablespoons almonds, slivered (sub chopped brazil
   or pine nuts or sunflower seeds)
1-1/2 to 2 lbs. fish fillets (see p.168)
1 tablespoon lemon juice
1 tsp. tarragon, crushed
Dash of cayenne
1/2 cup chopped mushrooms if desired

Heat oil in a large skillet. Add nuts and sauté over a
medium heat 2 to 3 minutes until golden brown, stirring
constantly. Remove nuts and set aside. In remaining oil,
cook fish 3 to 4 minutes on each side until fish flakes
when pierced with a fork. Remove to a warm platter and
season with salt and pepper. Stir remaining ingredients
into pan drippings with nuts and spoon over fish.

Even more simple;
Sprinkle fish with *tasty topping*; sauté until tender.

FISH WITH A K.I.S.S -- con't --

Like it crispy?
Sprinkle with tasty topping (see p.p.), coat with ground almonds, brazil nuts, or sunflower seeds; bake or fry until golden brown.

OR----try this.....
Baked fillets: Rinse fish, place in greased baking dish. Sprinkle with tasty topping or above seasonings, bake in preheated hot oven (400 F) about 20 minutes.

Serve with tossed green or grated carrot salad, and baked potato.

MEALS WITH A K.I.S.S.

(Keep It Simple, Sweetie)

Bake or fry a potato, steam a fresh vegetable*, (or place frozen vegetable in small saucepan), cover and heat slowly while steaming or sautéing fish.

Sprinkle with Tasty Topping and enjoy.

* carrots, artichokes, peppers, yams, jicama or mushrooms

TURKEY AND MUSHROOM BAKE

Yield: 6 portions   Preheat Oven: 375°

2 - 10 oz. packages frozen carrots *
1 cup sliced mushrooms
4 tablespoons potato flour**
2 cups turkey broth
1 lb. cooked turkey, cubed
1/2 cup chopped almonds, brazil nuts or sunflower seeds
2 tablespoons butter, melted

**See thickeners, p.26

Preheat oven to 375°. Cook carrots until just tender following package directions. Mix thickener and turkey broth in a shaker, so that it does not lump. Cook over a medium heat until thickened and smooth. Season to taste.

Place carrot pieces and mushrooms in a baking dish and cover with turkey. Pour gravy mixture over the turkey and carrots. Combine chopped nuts and melted butter and sprinkle on top. Bake uncovered 20 to 25 minutes until bubbly and browned.

Rabbit may be substituted for turkey.

* Fresh is always best. May also use parsley, potatoes, bell peppers, artichokes, jicama, or yams.

SUMMER GARDEN TURKEY
Yield: 8 portions   Preheat Oven: 325°

1 turkey hindquarter roast (3 to 6 lbs.)
1/4 cup sunflower, almond or apricot oil
1/2 teaspoon each: oregano, basil & tarragon
Salt and pepper to taste
2 cups carrots, mushrooms, peppers
    or artichoke hearts, lightly steamed.

Place turkey in shallow roasting pan. Combine oil and spices; baste turkey. Roast for 1-1/2 to 2-1/2 hours, depending on the size (or see crock pot cookery, p.p.) When done a meat thermometer registers 180 degrees F.. Combine the remaining dressing with the vegetables (any variety you prefer). Arrange vegetables on a platter. Top with turkey roast and serve.

TURKEY STROGANOFF
Yield: 8 portions

2 tablespoons sunflower or almond oil
1 lb. turkey, chopped or ground
1 lb. sliced mushrooms
1 sprig of parsley, chopped
1 chopped green pepper
1 cup turkey broth
1 teaspoon salt (opt)
1/4 teaspoon pepper

Heat oil in a wide frying pan over medium to high heat. Lightly brown turkey, just as turkey begins to brown add

TURKEY STROGANOFF, con't ---

mushrooms and peppers, sauté' about 3 minutes. Add broth, salt, pepper and thyme and simmer, stirring often, for about 5 minutes. Serve over rice, millet or potatoes. Garnish with fresh parsley.

VEGGIE NUT LOAF

1 cup carrots, grated
1 cup grated raw yams
1 cup finely chopped parsley
1/2 cup green pepper, finely chopped
1 cup ground almonds, brazil or pine nuts,
    or sunflower seeds
1 cup almond or sunflower butter
1 tsp. anise seed or coriander
Salt to taste

Stir nut butter until smooth; toss remaining ingredients together, then stir in the nut butter and mix well; press into a loaf pan or serving dish. Top with sprouts or chopped nuts; chill (overnight is best) and slice.

Try some of these variations:

Form into patties and make veggie burgers;
Roll into little balls and add to salads, or serve in pita bread;
Mash and spread on a rice cake or use as a sandwich filling.
Stuff celery, use as an appetizer.

CRACKERS & PIE CRUSTS

Made From Flour:
2 cups rice, millet, rye, yam, or potato flour
1 teaspoon baking powder or soda
1 teaspoon salt
1/3 cup sunflower or almond or apricot oil
1/3 cup cold water (approximate measure)

Made From Nuts Or Seeds:
2 cups nut or seed meal (see p.27) almond, brazil,
    or pine nuts; or sunflower seeds
1 tsp. baking powder
1 tsp. salt (opt)
1/3 cup thickener (flax seed meal or xanthan gum)

Hint: Oil is not usually needed with nuts and seeds. If the finished product is tough, add 1/8 cup oil the next time.

Combine flour, baking powder or soda and salt. Mix well, add oil and mix with a fork until crumbly. Add water slowly, as needed, form into 2 balls. Chill thoroughly.

PIE CRUST:

Roll chilled dough to 1/4" thick, fold and place into pie pan, or place ball in pan and press into place, flute edge as desired. Prick with fork. Bake at 350° for approximately 15 minutes, cool and add filling. Chill before serving.

See next page ->

Hint: Instead of trying to roll out the bottom crust, toss the ball in a greased (sprayed is even better) pie pan or dish; pat it flat with your fingers - gently coax the dough into a 1/8" thick crust. Even-out the lumps with a flat-bottomed glass.

Hint - When you create a crust you really love, double the recipe. The dough keeps up to 2 weeks refrigerated.

CRACKERS   Preheat Oven: 350°

Place ball on lightly greased baking sheet, roll out to about 1/4" thick. Dust dough with flour if necessary to keep from sticking to rolling pin. cut into 2" squares. Prick with fork all over. Bake in middle of preheated oven 350° for 10 minutes or until brown. (Time varies depending on type of flour used.) Watch carefully to prevent burning.

Create Fun Shapes - hearts, circles, animals - with cookie cutters, or cut into diamonds or 2" strips.

Variations: Sprinkle with chopped nuts, seeds or finely chopped dried fruit; roll again before cutting into squares.

Or try adding 1/2 tsp. seasoning, choose from: angelica, anise, caraway, chervil, dill seed & dill weed,   parsley.

Save Crumbs from broken and odd-shapes, crumble and use for cracker or bread crumbs, for croutons, stuffings, etc.

BASIC MUFFINS

Preheat Oven: 350°

Yield: 12 lg. or 18 small* muffins

2 cups flour (rice, millet, rye, or potato)
    or 1&1/2 cups meal (almond, brazil, sunflower) plus
    1/2 cup flax seed meal
1/2 teaspoon salt (optional)
1 egg or substitute (see p.23)
1/3 cup sunflower, almond or apricot oil
1 cup nut milk: almond, brazil, pine or sunflower
    or juice: apricot, prune, orange or berry.

Sift dry ingredients together. Mix wet ingredients
together well. Combine with dry ingredients, stirring until
just blended, do not over beat. Fill greased muffin cups*
1/2 full. Bake in preheated 350° oven for 12 to 15
minutes.

Just for fun - try some of these tasty variations:
Orange Spice:
Use orange juice for liquid, plus add 1 teaspoon grated
organic orange or lemon peel, and 1/2 teaspoon allspice
Carob Nut: Increase liquid to 1-1/4 cups. Add 1/2 cup
carob powder, 1/2 cup finely chopped nuts (almonds,
brazil, pine, or sunflower seeds), and/or 1/2 cup chopped
dates.

Hint: Place nuts on top of uncooked batter and they
won't sink to the bottom. *To avoid the dreaded *soggy
middle syndrome,* use small muffins tins.

NUTRI OLA

Cereal -- Breakfast Bar -- Snack Bar
Yield: 10 portions   Preheat Oven: 275°

2 cups rice, millet, rye or potato flour or -
  finely ground almonds, brazil nuts or sunflower seeds.
1 cup coarsely ground almonds, pine nuts or brazil nuts
1 cup whole sunflower seeds
1 cup finely chopped, dried dates, prunes, kiwi, guava, or
  apricots
1/2 cup molasses, rice syrup, date sugar or fruit puree
2 teaspoons pure almond extract

Preheat oven to 275°. Use a blender and or food
processor to grind nuts, grains or seeds to desired
consistency. Mix the nuts, seeds and/or grains in a large
bowl. Mix fruit, sweetener, and almond extract together.
Pour over the dry mixture and stir gently. Spread mixture
in a lightly oiled baking pan (15 x 10 x 1"). Bake for 1/2
hour stirring every 10 minutes. Cool. Break into small
pieces for cereal or large chunks for snacks. Store in
labeled container. This recipe makes approximately 6
cups.

Nutri Ola Snack Bars
Add to basic recipe - 2 eggs (or egg substitute), slowly
add additional liquid (water or juice) to make a stiff
batter. Follow above directions, bake at 350 F about 30
minutes, cut into squares.

Hint: Taste batter before baking, make sure you like it.
Add more sweetener or salt if desired.

PANCAKES made from flour

1-1/2 cups flour (rice, millet, rye, or potato)
  or 1 & 1/2 cups meal (almond, brazil, sunflower) plus
      1/2 cup flax seed meal
1/4 teaspoon salt
1 tablespoon baking powder
1 egg (or substitute, see p.23)
1-3/4 cups liquid: (almond, brazil, pine or sunflower milk)
or   (apricot, prune, orange or berry juice)
1 tsp. sunflower, almond, or apricot oil
1 tablespoon molasses (optional)

Combine dry ingredients and mix well. Combine egg,
liquid, oil and honey and add to dry ingredients. Bake on
preheated, non- stick griddle, turn when browned and
bubbly.

Hint: If batter thickens, add small amounts of liquid as
needed. Cool on wire rack so they don't stick together.

Double the Recipe: Use extras as a bread substitute.

Great for Lunches:
Make multi-layered sandwiches, or spread with fillings
and roll them up jelly roll fashion (like crepes or burritos).

Use your imagination for fillings, anything goes. (See
lunch suggestions).

PANCAKES made from nuts or seeds

1 & 1/2 cups meal (almond, brazil, sunflower) plus 1/2 cup   flax seed meal
1 teaspoon baking powder or soda
1 teaspoon salt (optional)
1/3 cup liquid: (almond, brazil, pine nut or sunflower milk) or   apricot, prune, orange or berry juice.
1 egg or substitute (see p.23)

Combine dry ingredients together and mix well. Combine liquid and egg and gently mix with dry ingredients. Bake on pre-heated, non-stick griddle.

Hint: If batter thickens, add small amounts of liquid as needed. Cool on wire rack so they don't stick together.

Double the Recipe: Use extras as a bread substitute.

Great for Lunches:
Make multi-layered sandwiches, or spread with fillings and roll them up jelly roll fashion (like crepes or burritos).

Use your imagination for fillings, anything goes. (See lunch suggestions).

Kid Pleasers:
Build multi-level sandwiches with a variety of fillings, or spread with filling and roll up jelly-roll fashion like crepes or burritos.

WONDERFUL WAFFLES *made with flour*

1-1/2 cups flour (rice, millet, rye, or potato)
1/4 teaspoon salt
1 tablespoon baking powder
1 egg (or substitute, see p.p.)
1-3/4 cups liquid: (almond, brazil, pine or sunflower milk)
or   (apricot, prune, orange or berry juice)
1/8 cup sesame, soy or walnut oil
1 tablespoon molasses (optional)

Combine dry ingredients , mix well. Combine egg, liquid,
oil and molasses together, mix and add to dry
ingredients. Bake in **pre-heated,** greased or sprayed
waffle iron, *with a **non-stick surface.** This is important!
Heavy flours tend to stick.* Otherwise, you'll be scraping
off the waffle in bits and pieces, cursing me --- not a good
way to start the day.

WONDERFUL WAFFLES - *made with nuts or seeds*

1 & 1/2 cups meal (almond, brazil, sunflower) plus
    1/2 cup flax seed meal
1 teaspoon baking powder or soda
1 teaspoon salt, (optional)
1/3 cup liquid: (almond, brazil, pine or sunflower milk) or
(apricot, prune, orange or berry juice) See p.p.
1/4 cup sunflower, almond or apricot oil
1 egg or substitute (see p.23)

Use the same mixing and baking instructions as above.

HEAVENLY NUT BREAD

Moist and wonderful!   *Pre-heat oven 350°F.*

2 cups flour (rice, millet, rye, or potato) - or -
   1 & 1/2 cups meal (almond, brazil, sunflower)
   plus 1/2 cup flax seed meal
1-1/2 teaspoons baking soda
1/2 teaspoon salt, if desired
1/2 teaspoon cinnamon
1/2 teaspoon nutmeg
1 cup chopped dates
1 cup chopped nuts; almonds, brazil, or sunflower seeds
1 cup fruit puree, molasses or rice syrup
1 cup orange, prune or cranberry juice
3 eggs or substitute, (see p.23)
1-1/2 cups yams, (cooked and pureed)
1-1/2 teaspoons almond extract

Combine dry ingredients together and mix well.
Combine wet ingredients together and mix well.
Gradually and gently blend wet and dry ingredients
together. Batter will be very thick. Spread in oiled and
floured pans and bake at 350° for about 1 hour until a
knife or toothpick inserted in the middle comes out clean.

NUT BUTTER COOKIES

Quick to fix - & a family favorite
Preheat Oven: 350° Yield: 2-1/2 doz.

1 cup nut butter (almond, brazil, or sunflower seed)
1/2 cup molasses or date sugar
1/8 cup sunflower, almond or apricot oil
1/2 teaspoon almond extract
1/4 teaspoon salt (optional)
2 cups flour (rice, millet, rye, or potato)
    or 1 & 1/2 cups meal (almond, brazil, sunflower) plus
    1/2 cup flax seed meal

Mix nut butter, sweetener and oil together until smooth.
Add flavoring and salt and blend again. Add flour or
starch a little at a time and mix well. *Mix flour in with
hands, not an electric mixer!* Roll dough into balls, place
on oiled cookie sheet, & flatten with a fork. **Or** form into
2" rolls on waxed paper. Chill and then slice 1/2" thick.

Bake about 12 minutes, **watch closely** to avoid
burning.
Uncooked dough keeps well in refrigerator. Bake as
needed. Freezes nicely also.

The following two recipes - "uncandies" - are great for
snacks any time of the day and are excellent travelers.

Added 1 egg
Molasses cookies 1/2 t. cinnamon
1/2 t. ginger
1/4 t. cloves

APRICOT - ALMOND BARS

2 cups dried seedless fruit
  (prunes or apricots)
2 cups nut or seed meal
1/4 teaspoon salt (optional)
1/2 teaspoon almond extract

Food Processor: Cut fruit into small pieces, toss into
the food processor; add nuts or seeds, salt and extract,
blend until ball forms. Use the metal chopping blade.
Blender: Cut up fruit, place in blender and chop fine.
Chop nuts separately, mix with fruit. Use sturdy spoon to
mix and knead, or use fingers. If too dry to mix well, a
small amount of water or juice. Batter will be *very* stiff
Press firmly into oiled pie pan or cookie sheet, cut in
squares; or place on waxed paper; form into 2" roll - or in
little balls - roll in additional chopped nuts or seeds; .
Wrap logs in waxed paper or foil (shiny side next to
food). chill and slice as needed. Store in refrigerator.

NUT BUTTER uncandy *CANDY*

1 cup nut butter (almond, brazil or sunflower seed)
1 cup chopped dates
1/8 cup molasses, or to taste
1/2 cup chopped nuts (see above)

Toss into food processor; or use sturdy spoon to mix.
Follow the above mixing directions -- starting with ***Press***
firmly--

Notes -
Favorite combinations, etc. :

Notes –
Favorite combinations, etc. :

Day 3

Blue Day

FOODS FOR DAY 3

Strictly optional - Just ignore what you don't like or can't eat. And remember -- Day 1 and Day 3 foods are interchangeable.

Proteins
Fish can be eaten daily as long as a different fish is selected each day; Oysters, scallops, abalone; game hens, quail, pheasant; goat milk - yogurt &/or cheeses.

Legumes
Pinto, garbanzo & black beans, black-eyed & split peas. Nuts, seeds and oils
Chestnuts, peanuts, pecans, macadamia nuts, pumpkin seeds, olives and olive oil.

Grains, flours, misc.
Amaranth or quinoa, kudzu & garbanzo flour, kudzu root. **Bulking agent**: chia seed.

Vegetables
Spinach, bok choy, red radish, Brussels sprouts, cauliflower, summer squash, pumpkin, zucchini, chives, leeks, shallots, asparagus, peas, okra, olives, chestnuts.

Fruit
Pears, quince, pineapple, loganberries, raspberries, gooseberries, cantaloupe, & melons.

Sweeteners
Figs and currants; plus above fruits.

Spices:
Oregano, peppermint, rosemary, sage, savory, thyme, ginger, turmeric, licorice, senna, chives (fresh or dried).

TASTY TOPPING *Season Salt*

Preheat Oven: 325°

Sprinkle on hot or cold foods, veggies, snacks, etc.

1 cup ground pecans, macadamia nuts,
    or pumpkin seeds
1 tablespoon salt (optional)
1 clove shallots, minced
1 tablespoon poppy seeds
1 Tbsp. seasoning; choice of:
    oregano, peppermint, rosemary, sage, savory, thyme,
    ginger, turmeric, licorice, senna, chives (fresh or
    dried).

Toast nuts or seeds until light brown in 325° oven,
about
10 minutes. Stir to avoid burning. Place in blender,
grind
to a fine texture. Use in place of salt. Adds zest to boring
ole' vegetables, salads, or main dishes -- almost
anything.

Make a double batch and store in a glass jar
in the refrigerator.

Hint - SALT-FREE SPRINKLES
Follow above directions, omit salt, sprinkle on waffles,
pancakes, hot or cold cereals, etc.

NUT BUTTERS, SAUCES & MILKS

A 'butter' can be made out of any kind of seed or nut, or combination. Day 3: peanuts, pecans, macadamia nuts, pumpkin seeds
Use a seed/nut mill or grinder, coffee-bean grinder, blender, or a food processor (use the metal blade) to produce a fine flour, or *meal*. One cup of whole nuts or seeds yields about 1/2 cup of ground flour, or *meal*. See manufacturer's instructions.

NUT BUTTER: 1 cup meal blended with about 3 tablespoons of water or oil. Add sea salt to taste. Blend, or mix until smooth.

DIP OR SPREAD: Add liquid to butter recipe above to bring mixture to the desired consistency. Season to taste. Add chopped nuts or seeds as desired.

SAUCE OR SALAD DRESSING: Add liquid to desired consistency. Season to taste

NUT OR SEED MILK *(Designer Milks)*
1/4 cup nuts or seeds (see above) & 8 oz. water. Blend until smooth. Strain if desired. Add approximately 1 teaspoon honey **, raisin juice or fruit juice concentrate if desired. Use as a milk substitute.

*** Do NOT give honey to an infant under one year of age, due to chance of botulism poisoning.*

BASIC SALAD DRESSING

1 teaspoon salt (optional)
1/4 teaspoon black pepper
1 teaspoon oregano, savory or thyme
1/4 cup lime juice
2/3 cup olive or peanut oil

Place ingredients in blender until smooth; or mix well; store in refrigerator. Double the recipe for convenience.

Hint - For *THICK or CREAMY* dressing, add 1 tsp. guar or xanthan gum, mix well (see p.22)

CLAM SAUCE

1 clove shallots, crushed
1 leek, chopped fine
1/2 stick butter or 3 tablespoons oil
2 - 8 oz. cans minced clams, save juice
Sprouts, bean threads, or cooked amaranth or quinoa

Sauté garlic and onion in butter or oil. Add the juice from the clams and simmer about 20 minutes. Add the clams just before serving. Heat only long enough to make it good and hot. Serve over sprouts, noodles, cooked, whole grains.
To thicken sauce: mix 1 tsp. arrowroot with 1/4 cup cold water, add to juice and simmer as above.

CHOWDER:
Simply add a can of clam juice, serve with croutons made from crackers 'of the day'.

SLOW (CROCK POT) COOKING

Breakfast can be a snap by starting it at bedtime. (See *cooking whole grains)*

Oil the inside of the pot to prevent sticking. Add:
- 1 cup whole amaranth
- 2 cups water
- 1/2 cup cut-up dried pears, pineapple, currants and/or figs
- Pinch of salt, if desired

Turn on low before retiring. In the morning, add nut milk, if you want to, and enjoy.

Hint - Wash the pot after breakfast and start dinner:

Place a pork or lamb roast; or game hens or pheasant in the pot, add cut-up leeks, Brussels sprouts, okra, cauliflower, or zucchini. Dinner will be ready by 5 pm. Add peas or asparagus 30 minutes before serving.

Hint - Want meat or poultry for breakfast?

Place in pot before bedtime without vegetables. Have some for breakfast, &/or pack for your lunch . Then toss some vegetables in the pot, on top of the meat, and let simmer until lunch or dinner time.

Old fashioned bean or split pea soups are nourishing, and good to eat any time of day or night.

MARINATED VEGGIES

(Double recipe, it keeps well)

1/3 cup vinegar (sub pineapple juice or Vit C., see p.24)
1 or 2 cloves shallots, crushed
1 teaspoon dried salad herbs and seasonings
    Choice of: turmeric, oregano, mint, sage, savory &/or
    thyme
1/8 cup oil (olive, peanut, or pumpkin)
1 lb. (total) vegetables, and cooked beans
    Frozen veggies are OK, do not cook
1/2 teaspoon salt - optional

In a small saucepan combine vinegar, shallots and
herbs. Simmer very gently for about 5 minutes; add oil.
Cover and set aside to steep. Cut vegetables into bite-
size pieces. Hard vegetables such as Brussels sprouts,
cauliflower, okra, asparagus may be lightly steamed
first, while others such as zucchini, radishes, leeks,
peas or olives are best if left raw. Bite sized pieces of
left-over meats are delicious marinated, as are cooked
beans such as chick peas or pinto beans . Toss
vegetables &/or beans & salt in a large bowl. Pour
marinade evenly over the vegetables and toss again.
Let sit at least 1 hour, to develop full flavor; the flavor
gets richer each day.

Hint: Marinated veggies can be mixed into salads,
served as pickles or as a side dish. They make a nice
winter salad; a main dish; or delicious accompaniment
to grains, pasta and non-vegetarian main dishes.

BEAN SPROUT SALAD

Delightful, colorful and crunchy   Yield: 4 portions

1 quart (1/2 lb.) mung bean sprouts
1 large leek, thinly sliced
4 radishes, thinly sliced
1/3 small zucchini, unpeeled, thinly sliced
    (on the diagonal)
2 cans water chestnuts, sliced

Rinse bean sprouts. Drop into boiling water for 2
minutes and drain in colander. Immediately dip
colander into large pan of ice water to stop the cooking
process. Stir gently with a fork. When cold, remove
colander from water, drain. Dry on paper towel. Mix
remaining ingredients with sprouts, toss with basic
salad dressing (and a few drops of wheat-free soy
sauce, if tolerated); chill before serving.

ORIENTAL SPINACH SALAD

2 bunches of spinach
1/8 cup oil
1/4 cup vinegar (sub. Vit C, see p.24)
1 oz. mashed anchovy
1/2 lb. small, fresh shrimp

Cook spinach and rinse in ice cold water. Chop and mix
with remaining ingredients. Chill before serving.
Sprinkle with chopped pecans, macadamia nuts or
pumpkin seeds.

SASSY SPINACH SALAD

1 tablespoon chives, chopped
2 tablespoons leeks, diced
1/2 cup chopped radishes
1/2 cup olives, chopped
Salad dressing of your choice (see p.101)
16 oz. fresh spinach (1 bunch)

Mince chives, leeks, radishes and olives together until very fine and pulpy, set aside. Wash spinach, drain, tear into small pieces. Toss with dressing before serving. Garnish with bacon bits, chopped ham, chopped, roasted nuts or pumpkin seeds.

ZUCCHINI CRISP

2 or 3 small zucchini
1/2 teaspoon salt
1/2 cup salad dressing (see p.101)
1/4 cup chopped, toasted pumpkin seeds, macadamia
   nuts, pecans or olives
2 tablespoons minced chives

Cut zucchini into very thin slices. Mix together with all other ingredients and chill. Serve on a bed of crisp greens.

Garnish with bacon bits, chopped ham, chopped, roasted nuts or pumpkin seeds.

FESTIVE FISH SALAD

1 lb. cooked, firm fish - *canned fish is OK*
1/4 cup salad dressing (see p.101)
1 med. leek, chopped
6 sliced radishes
1 cup bite size pieces of cauliflower
1 cup steamed Brussels sprouts, quartered. *Frozen O.K.*
1/4 cup chopped green or ripe olives
3 cloves shallots, crushed
1 can sliced water chestnuts
1 cup cooked garbanzo or pinto beans
1 teaspoon seasoning, choose from: oregano,
    peppermint, rosemary, sage, savory, thyme, ginger,
    turmeric, licorice
1/8 cup olive, peanut or pumpkin oil   Salt to taste

Poach, drain and chill fish. See instructions, p.168. Cut
fish into bite-sized cubes and marinate with the other
ingredients at least 1 hour before serving. Serve on
crisp greens.

MOLDED SEAFOOD SALAD

1 tablespoon unflavored gelatin
1/4 cup cold water; & 1/2 cup boiling water
3/4 cups salad dressing (see p.p.)
1/2 cup each chopped zucchini, leeks, water chestnuts
10 green olives, chopped
1/2 teaspoon salt, if desired
1-1/2 cups chopped or flaked, cooked seafood

Molded Seafood Salad, con't --

Soak gelatin in cold water to soften, dissolve in hot water. Mix with dressing, combine with the remaining ingredients, pour
into greased mold and chill until firm. Serve on fresh greens - spinach or bok choy leaves.

PERKY PECAN VEGETABLES

4 cups steamed or frozen vegetables
Choice of:
    spinach, bok choy, red radish, Brussels sprouts,
    cauliflower, summer squash, pumpkin, zucchini,
    leeks, asparagus, peas &/or okra.
1 tablespoon unrefined olive or peanut oil
1/4 cup pecan or macadamia nuts or pumpkin seeds
Sea salt to taste (opt)

Cook vegetables until tender but crisp. Drain. Heat oil in skillet. Add pecan or macadamia nuts or pumpkin seeds and stir until sizzling. Add vegetables *carefully*, the oil may spatter; gently heat through. Season to taste.

MINESTRONE *Big Soup*

1/4 lb. dry beans
2 quarts water
4 tablespoons leeks, chopped
1 tablespoon olive or peanut oil
1/2 lb. zucchini, peeled and diced
1/4 lb. cut green string beans
3 cups chopped boy choy or cauliflower
1 shallot, crushed
Sea salt, to taste
1 tsp. seasonings, choose from:
    oregano, peppermint, rosemary, sage, savory, thyme,
    ginger, turmeric, chives (fresh or dried).

Pour boiling water over beans and let stand overnight.
Drain and then cook in 2 quarts of water for at least 4
hours. (See Basic Bean Cooking, p.166) Sauté leeks
and zucchini in olive oil for 5 minutes. Add to the beans.
Add remaining ingredients, and additional water if
needed. Cover and cook over a low heat at least one
hour.

Notes:

LIVELY LEEK SOUP

1 tablespoon oil or butter
3 cups chopped leeks
2 tablespoons flour (amaranth, bean, chestnut, or
   kudzu root.
4 cups water   Salt to taste
1 tsp. seasoning, choose from:
   oregano, rosemary, sage, savory, thyme, ginger,
   turmeric, chives (fresh or dried).

Sauté leeks in oil until brown. Blend in flour, gradually
stir in water. Add seasoning and salt, if desired, and
simmer over low heat, stirring occasionally, for 30
minutes. Serve hot. Tofu cubes, or chunks of cooked
seafood, poultry or meats may be added during the last
2 minutes of cooking.

SEAFOOD BOUILLON - Good Basic Stock

2 lbs. fish trimmings (see p.168)
2 quarts water
1 tsp. seasoning: oregano, peppermint, rosemary,
   sage, savory, thyme, ginger, turmeric or chives
1 Tbsp. oil or butter
1 large leek, sliced
1 clove shallots, diced
1 cup chopped spinach or zucchini
2 teaspoons salt

Sauté leek in butter or oil until brown, combine all
ingredients and simmer for 1 hour; strain. Refrigerate up
to 3 days, or freeze 'til needed.

FISH WITH A K.I.S.S. *Keep it Simple, Sweetie*

Yield: 6 portions

2 Tbsp. olive, peanut or pumpkin oil
3 Tbsp. macadamia nuts, pecans or pumpkin seeds
1-1/2 to 2 lbs. fish fillets (see p.168)
1 tablespoon vinegar or pineapple juice
1/2 teaspoon chives
1/4 teaspoon pepper
Salt to taste (optional)

Heat 2 tablespoons of oil in a large skillet. Add nuts and sauté over a medium heat 2 to 3 minutes until golden brown, stirring constantly. Remove nuts and set aside. In remaining oil, cook fish 3 to 4 minutes on each side until done. Remove to a warm platter and season with salt and pepper. Stir remaining ingredients into pan drippings with nuts and spoon over fish.

Even more simple;
Sprinkle fish with tasty topping and sauté'.

Like it crispy?
Sprinkle with tasty topping, coat with ground nuts or seeds (see above); bake or sauté' until golden brown.

Or - try this.....

Baked fillets: Rinse fish, place in greased baking dish. Sprinkle with tasty topping or above seasonings, bake in preheated hot oven (400 F) about 20 minutes.

Serve with spinach salad, steamed or stir- fry veggies, asparagus and/or baked squash or sweet potato.

VEGGIE BURGER Dujour #3

Great for breakfast!

1/2 cup leeks or chives, chopped
1/2 cup chopped pecans, macadamia nuts or
   pumpkin seeds
1/4 cup bean flour, or egg or egg substitute
1/2 teaspoon salt, if desired
1 clove shallots, chopped
2 cups cooked, mashed squash, pumpkin or beans

Combine all ingredients. Form into patties. If too dry, add water; if too moist, add additional flour or nut meal to desired consistency. Sauté' in lightly oiled (or sprayed) skillet until browned nicely on both sides.

This is a wonderful, versatile patty. Travels well, great for lunches for school, or to work, or outings. Easy to mass-produce. Make ahead of time and freeze for future use.

VEGGIE NUT LOAF

1 cup zucchini, grated
1/2 cup grated pears or drained, crushed pineapple
1/2 cup (1 small can, drained) chopped black olives
1 cup alfalfa sprouts, chopped
1 clove shallots, minced (optional)
1 cup finely ground macadamias, pecans or pumpkin
   seeds.
Salt to taste

Combine everything, mold into an oiled loaf pan. Top with sprouts, chill (overnight is best) and slice.

SUMMER GARDEN GAME HEN

Yield: 8 lg. portions Preheat Oven: 325°

4 game hens
1/4 cup sunflower, almond or apricot oil
1/2 teaspoon oregano
1/2 teaspoon basil
1/2 teaspoon tarragon
Salt and pepper to taste
4 cups lightly steamed vegetables: Brussels sprouts, cauliflower, zucchini, asparagus, peas, okra, or squash. *Any combination that strikes your fancy.*

Combine oil and spices; place game hens in a shallow roasting pan, baste; bake until golden brown - about 1 hour, depending on size of the hens. When done a meat thermometer registers 180 degrees F.

About 10 minutes before the hens are done, steam vegetables and toss with remaining dressing. Arrange vegetables on a platter. Top with game hens and serve.

VARIATION:
Place 1 cup whole amaranth or quinoa, and 2 cups water in roasting pan, add hens; baste. As hens roast, the tasty 'drippings' season the grain.

Hint -

Try this method on different days, using the grain or poultry assigned to that day. For instance, turkey wings and rice are a tasty combination for Day 2..

KOREAN LAMB OR PORK (Kun Koki)

Great company dish   *Yield: 6-8 portions*

2 lbs. lamb or pork steaks or chops

Marinade:
1/4 cup olive or peanut oil
1/2 teaspoon salt
2 cloves shallots, minced or crushed
1/2 teaspoon black pepper
1/2 teaspoon ginger
1/4 cup pineapple juice
1 leek, thinly sliced, or chopped chives

Score steak or chops and place in glass dish. Combine other ingredients and marinate steak or chops at least 2 hours, overnight is better.

Broil about 5 minutes per side on preheated grill or under broiler. Lamb may be served rare, but pork needs to be cooked until well done.

PORK OR LAMB STROGANOFF

Yield: 8 portions

1 lb. pork or lamb, chopped or ground
2 tablespoons peanut, pumpkin or olive oil
1 medium leek, chopped (optional)
1 clove shallots, minced or pressed
1 cup pork or lamb broth (or bouillon)
1 teaspoon salt
1/4 teaspoon pepper
Chives, chopped

Heat oil in a wide frying pan over medium to high heat.
Lightly brown meat. Just as meat begins to brown add
leek and shallots, stirring until limp. Add broth, salt,
pepper and spices; simmer, stirring often, for about 5
minutes. Thicken with guar or xanthan gum (see p. 22).

Serve over cooked amaranth, quinoa &/or vegetables.
Any combination of: cooked cauliflower, Brussels
sprouts, zucchini, asparagus, spinach, okra, or cubed or
mashed squash.

Or, just for fun -
Make a 'boat' out of a cooked, halved acorn or zucchini
squash, (sliced lengthwise); fill with stroganoff mixture
and serve hot.

Garnish with chopped chives &/or chopped nuts.

CREATIVE CURRIED LAMB

Yield: 6 portions

1 pound cubed lamb
1 teaspoon salt
1/2 teaspoon pepper
1 to 2 tablespoons olive, peanut, or pumpkin oil
3/4 teaspoon curry powder
1/4 teaspoon powdered ginger
1-1/2 cups water
3 bouillon cubes, crumbled
1-1/2 tablespoons amaranth or bean flour, or kudzu root
3 tablespoons lime juice

Season lamb with salt and pepper. In a heavy skillet, brown meat slowly on both sides using just enough oil to prevent sticking. Add curry powder and ginger and sauté slowly for 5 minutes. Stir in water and bouillon cubes. Cover and simmer 1 hour or until lamb is tender.

Remove lamb and keep warm. Skim off and discard any fat from juices. Blend thickener with 1/4 cup cold water. Stir into liquid remaining in pan. Cook, stirring until sauce boils and thickens slightly. Stir in the lime juice.

Serve lamb with thickened pan juices on the side.

Add whole grain amaranth or quinoa and a platter of steamed veggies for a festive meal.

MEALS WITH A K.I.S.S.
Keep It Simple, Sweetie

Steam a fresh vegetable*, or toss some frozen vegetables in a saucepan, cover and heat slowly while steaming or sautéing some fresh fish.

Sprinkle with Tasty Topping - enjoy.

* spinach, bok choy, Brussels sprouts, cauliflower, squash, zucchini, asparagus, peas or okra.

Tips And Tricks About Baking With "Weird" Grains.
The following recipes are pretty basic, and allow you to choose what type of grain or ground nuts for each recipe.

Choose a basic pancake recipe and make it with the ingredients you are allowed to have in your menu plan, experiment until you get it just to your liking, not too thick or thin. When you've found a few favorites, double the recipes and freeze 'til needed.

Hint - Forget what your elders said years ago, and learn to *play with your food*. Create taste tempting dishes with a variety of fillings and spreads.

CRACKERS & PIE CRUSTS

MADE FROM FLOUR:
2 cups amaranth, chestnut, squash or bean flour
1 teaspoon baking powder or soda
1 teaspoon salt
1/3 cup olive, peanut or pumpkin oil or goat butter
1/3 cup cold water (approximate measure)

MADE FROM NUTS OR SEEDS:
2 cups pecan, macadamia or pumpkin seed meal
1 tsp. baking powder
1 tsp. salt (opt)
1/3 cup thickener (Kudzu root or see above)

NOTE: Oil is not usually needed with nuts and seeds. If finished product is too tough, add oil next time.

Combine flour, baking powder or soda and salt. Mix well, add oil and mix with a fork until crumbly. Add water slowly, as needed, form into 2 balls. Chill thoroughly.

PIE CRUST:

Roll chilled dough to 1/4" thick, fold and place into pie pan, or place ball in pan and press into place, flute edge as desired. Prick with fork. Bake at 350° for approximately 15 minutes, cool and add filling. Chill before serving.

See next page ->

PIE CRUST, con't --

Hint: Instead of trying to roll out the bottom crust, toss the ball in a greased (sprayed is even better) pie pan or dish; pat it flat with your fingers - gently coax the dough into a 1/8" thick crust. Even-out the lumps with a flat-bottomed glass.

Hint - When you create a crust you really love, double the recipe. The dough keeps up to 2 weeks refrigerated.

CRACKERS   Preheat Oven: 350°

Place ball on lightly greased baking sheet, roll out to about 1/4" thick. Dust dough with flour if necessary to keep from sticking to rolling pin. cut into 2" squares. Prick with fork all over. Bake in middle of preheated oven 350° for 10 minutes or until brown. (Time varies depending on type of flour used.) Watch carefully to prevent burning.

Variations: **Create Fun Shapes** - hearts, circles, animals - with cookie cutters, or cut into diamonds or 2" strips.
Sprinkle with chopped nuts, seeds or finely chopped dried fruit; roll again before cutting into squares.

Or, add 1/2 tsp. seasoning, choose from: oregano, peppermint, rosemary, sage, savory, thyme, ginger, turmeric, licorice, chives (fresh or dried).

Save Crumbs from broken and odd-shapes, crumble and use for cracker or bread crumbs, for croutons, stuffings, etc.

PANCAKES made from flour

1-1/2 cups flour (amaranth, chestnut, or garbanzo)
1/4 teaspoon salt
1 tablespoon baking powder
1 egg (or substitute, see p.23)
1-3/4 cups liquid: nut milk (pecan, peanut, or
    macadamia) or juice: (pear, pineapple or berry)
1 Tbsp. pumpkin, peanut or olive oil

Combine dry ingredients and mix well. Combine egg,
liquid, oil and add to dry ingredients. Bake on preheated, non-stick griddle, turn when browned and
bubbly.

Note: If batter thickens, add small amounts of liquid as
needed.

Double the Recipe: Use extras as a bread substitute.
Cool on wire rack so they don't stick together.

Hint - Great for Lunches:

Make multi-layered sandwiches, or spread with fillings
and roll them up jelly roll fashion (like crepes or
burritos).

Use your imagination for fillings, anything goes. (See
lunch suggestions).

PANCAKES made from nuts or seeds

1-1/2 cups meal: pecan, macadamia, pumpkin seed or
   peanut - plus 1/2 cup thickener
1 teaspoon baking powder or soda
1 teaspoon salt (optional)
1/3 count milk: (pecan, peanut, or macadamia;
   or juice: pear, pineapple or berry
1 tsp. pumpkin, peanut or olive oil
1 egg or substitute (see p.23)

Combine dry ingredients together and mix well.
Combine liquid and egg and gently mix with dry
ingredients. Bake on pre-heated, non-stick griddle.

Hint: If batter thickens, add small amounts of liquid as
needed.
Cool the cakes on a wire rack so they don't stick
together.
Double the Recipe: Use the extra pancakes like flat
bread.

Hint - Kid Pleasers:
Build multi-level sandwiches with a variety of fillings, or
spread with filling and roll up jelly-roll fashion like
crepes or burritos.

WONDERFUL WAFFLES *made with flour*

1-1/2 cups flour (amaranth, chestnut, or garbanzo)
1/4 teaspoon salt
1 tablespoon baking powder
1 egg (or substitute, see p.23)
1-3/4 cups nut milk: pecan, peanut, or macadamia;
    or juice: pear, pineapple or berry.
1/4 cup pumpkin, peanut or olive oil*

Combine dry ingredients, mix well. Combine egg,
liquid, and oil; mix and add to dry ingredients. Bake in
hot waffle iron (non- stick).

WONDERFUL WAFFLES -
made with nuts or seeds

1 & 1/2 cups meal - pecan, macadamia, pumpkin seed
    or peanut, plus 1/2 cup thickener
1 teaspoon baking powder or soda
1 teaspoon salt, (optional)
1/3 cup nut milk: pecan, peanut, or macadamia:
    or juice: pear, pineapple or berry
1/4 cup pumpkin, peanut or olive oil*
1 egg or substitute (see p.23)

Use the same mixing and baking instructions as above.

Hint: *You can try less oil if you like - problem is - the
waffle will stick and you'll have to scrape it off in tiny
pieces.

BUOYANT BEAN PANCAKES

From: Pauline Adams

2 eggs or egg sub (see p.23)
3/4 cup water
1/2 cup bean flour
1/4 teaspoon salt (optional)
1/2 teaspoon soda
1/2 cup chopped nuts (optional)
   (pecans, macadamia nuts or peanuts)

Mix together egg substitute and water, let stand about 10 minutes. Combine bean flour, salt, soda and chopped nuts; add to wet mixture and let stand until mixture thickens. Cook on a pre-heated non-stick surface for best results. When done, transfer to warm platter, and sprinkle with cheese (if allowed) or any other topping (like refried beans or nut butter), and place in a warm oven until served

Hint: For an even lighter 'cake', mix the night before & omit soda; Just before baking, add soda; then add additional liquid as needed. Bean and other heavy flours yield a finer finished product the longer they 'soak', freezing uncooked batter further improves texture.

Hint: Double or even triple this recipe, cool on wire rack, or place towels in between until cool so they won't stick together. Store in refrigerator or freezer for future use as sandwich material. Add ground or chopped nuts or seeds for variety. Package as individual servings and freeze for lunches and travel.

NUTRI OLA

Cereal -- Breakfast Bar -- Snack Bar
Yield: 10 portions   Preheat Oven: 275°

2 cups amaranth, chestnut, or garbanzo flour; or finely
    ground pecans, macadamia nuts or pumpkin seeds
1 cup coarsely ground pecans or macadamia nuts
1 cup coarsely chopped pumpkin seeds
1 cup finely chopped dried figs, currants, pears or
    pineapple
1/2 cup puree from above fruits or
    concentrated fruit juice
1/4 cup olive, peanut or pumpkin oil
2 teaspoons vanilla

Preheat oven to 275°. Use a blender and or food
processor to grind nuts, grains or seeds to desired
consistency. Mix the nuts, seeds and/or grains in a
large bowl. Mix together with fruit and sweetener, oil
and vanilla. Pour over the dry mixture and stir lightly.
Spread mixture in a lightly oiled baking pan (15 x 10 x
1"). Bake for 1/2 hour stirring every 10 minutes. Cool.
Break into small pieces for cereal or large chunks for
snacks. Store in labeled container. This recipe makes
approximately 6 cups.

NUTRI OLA SNACK BARS

Add to basic recipe - 2 eggs (or egg substitute), slowly add additional liquid (water or juice) to make a stiff batter. Follow above directions, bake at 350 F about 30 minutes, cut into squares.

Hint -Taste batter before baking, make sure you like it. Add more sweetener or salt if desired.

Notes -

BASIC MUFFINS   Preheat Oven: 350°

Yield: 12 large or 18 small* muffins

2 cups flour (amaranth, chestnut, or garbanzo)
   Or 1 & 1/2 cups meal (pecan, macadamia, pumpkin
   seed or peanut, **plus** 1/2 cup kudzu root) see p.26.
1 teaspoon baking powder
1/2 teaspoon salt (optional)
1 egg or substitute, see p.p.
1/8 cup pumpkin, peanut or olive oil
1 cup nut milk: pecan, peanut, or macadamia,
   or juice: pear, pineapple or berry

Sift dry ingredients together. Mix wet ingredients
together well. Combine with dry ingredients, stirring
until just blended, do not over beat. Fill greased muffin
cups 1/2 full. Bake in preheated 400° oven for 12 to 15
minutes.

Just for fun - try some of these tasty variations:

PUMPKIN SPICE: add 1 cup cooked pumpkin in
place of liquid, 1/2 teaspoon nutmeg, ginger and/or
allspice.
PINEAPPLE NUT: add 1 8 oz. can of drained,
crushed pineapple, 1/2 cup of the juice in place of
liquid, and a dash of nutmeg if desired.

Hint: Place nuts on top of uncooked batter and they
won't sink to the bottom. *To avoid the dreaded *soggy
middle syndrome,* use small muffins tins.

NUT BUTTER COOKIES

Quick to fix - & a family favorite

Preheat Oven: 350° Yield: 2-1/2 doz.

1 cup nut butter (pecan, peanut or macadamia)
1/2 cup fig or currant, or fruit puree or concentrated
   pineapple juice.
1/8 cup olive, pumpkin or peanut oil
1/2 teaspoon vanilla
1/4 teaspoon salt (optional)
2 cups flour (amaranth, chestnut, or garbanzo)
Or nut meal (pecan, macadamia, pumpkin seed
   or peanut [if tolerated])

Mix nut butter, sweetener and oil together until smooth.
Add flavoring and salt and blend again. Add flour or
starch a little at a time and mix well. (It's usually best to
mix flour in with hands, not an electric mixer)

Roll dough into balls, place on oiled cookie sheet, &
flatten with a fork. **Or** form into 2" rolls on waxed paper.
Chill and slice 1/2" thick.

Bake about 12 minutes, **watch closely** to avoid
burning.

Hint - Uncooked dough keeps well in refrigerator.

Bake as needed. Freezes nicely also.

HEAVENLY NUT BREAD
Moist and wonderful!   *Pre-heat oven 350°F.*

2 cups flour (amaranth, chestnut, or garbanzo)
   Or 1 & 1/2 cups meal (pecan, macadamia, pumpkin
   seed or peanut - **plus** 1/2 cup thickener (see p.22)
1-1/2 teaspoons baking soda
1/2 teaspoon salt, optional
1/2 tsp. each - powdered ginger & ground cardamom
1 cup currants
1/2 cup chopped pecans
3/4 cup pumpkin, peanut or olive oil
1 cup fruit puree or ground figs
1 cup pineapple juice
3 eggs or substitute, see p.p.
1-1/2 cups pumpkin (cooked or pureed)
1-1/2 teaspoons vanilla

Combine dry ingredients together and mix well.
Combine wet ingredients together and mix well.
Gradually and gently blend wet and dry ingredients
together. Batter will be very thick.
Spread in oiled and floured pans bake at 350° for about
1 hour until a toothpick inserted in the middle comes out
clean.

PINEAPPLE NUT BREAD

Substitute one 4 oz. can crushed pineapple for the
pumpkin, increase pecans to 1 cup, and omit currants.

Hint: To avoid the dreaded *soggy middle syndrome*,
use small pans rather than large pans.

TROPICAL FRUIT & NUT BARS

No cooking required

2 cups dried fruit: pineapple, pears, figs or currants
2 cups nut or seed meal
1/4 teaspoon salt (optional)
1/2 teaspoon flavoring, if desired.

Food Processor: Cut fruit into small pieces, toss into
the food processor; add nuts or seeds, blend until ball
forms. Use the metal chopping blade.

Blender: Cut up fruit, place in blender and chop fine.
Chop nuts separately, mix with fruit. Use sturdy spoon
to mix and knead, or use fingers. If too dry to mix well, a
small amount of water or juice. Batter will be *very* stiff

Press firmly into oiled pie pan or cookie sheet, cut in
squares; or place on waxed paper; form into 2" roll - or
in little balls - roll in additional chopped nuts or seeds; .
Wrap logs in waxed paper or foil (shiny side next to
food). chill and slice as needed. Store in refrigerator.

NUT BUTTER uncandy *CANDY*

1 cup nut butter (pecan, macadamia, or peanut)
1/2 cup finely chopped nuts (see above)
1/4 cup carob powder
1/2 cup ground figs or currants

Toss into food processor; or use sturdy spoon to mix.
Follow the above mixing directions -- starting with
Press *firmly--*

Day 4

Red Day

DAY 4 FOOD CHOICES

Day 2 and Day 4 foods and recipes are interchangeable. You may switch them back and forth, just remember to wait for four days before eating that food again.

Proteins
Fish may be eaten daily as long as a different fish is selected each day; crab, squid, octopus; duck & duck eggs; rabbit.

Nuts, seeds and oils
Cashews, pistachio nuts; safflower, corn and avocado oil.

Grains and flours
Barley, corn, kamut, oats, teff, wheat, tapioca, agar agar, psyllium seed.

Vegetables
Avocado, parsnips, celery, iceberg lettuce, romaine, tomatoes, eggplant, peppers, bamboo shoots, Jerusalem artichokes, sweet potatoes.

Fruits
Peach, cherry, nectarine, lime, grapefruit, tangerine, blueberry, pomegranate, mango, banana.

Sweeteners
Coconut, malt, sago palm, maple syrup; fruits & fruit juice - use frozen juice diluted or full strength.

Seasonings
Chili, bell peppers, fennel, celery seed & leaves, cilantro, cumin.

TASTY TOPPING *Season Salt*
Preheat Oven: 375°

Sprinkle on hot or cold foods, veggies, snacks, etc.

1 cup finely chopped cashews or pistachios
1 tablespoon salt (optional)
1 Tbsp. seasonings - choose from: dried bell peppers,
  chili powder, fennel, celery seed & leaves, cilantro,
  cumin.

Mix all ingredients together, sprinkle onto large flat pan.

Bake 350° F, 10-15 minutes. Stir often. Make a double
batch and store in a glass jar in the refrigerator.

CASHEW SPRINKLES * *Preheat Oven: 325°*

1 cup cashews or pistachios
1 teaspoon salt

Toast nuts or seeds until light brown in 325° oven, about
10 minutes. Stir to avoid burning. Place in blender, grind
to a fine texture. Use in place of salt. Adds zest to boring
ole' vegetables, salads, or main dishes -- almost
anything.

SALT-FREE SPRINKLES
Follow above directions, omit salt, sprinkle on waffles,
pancakes, hot or cold cereals, etc.

BASIC SALAD DRESSING

1 teaspoon salt (optional)
1/4 teaspoon cayenne pepper
or dash of tobasco
1 teaspoon dry parsley or dill weed
1/4 cup vinegar (sub. Vit. C, see p.24)
2/3 cup safflower, corn or avocado oil

Mix well, store in refrigerator. Double - or even triple -
the recipe for convenience.

Hint - For *THICK or CREAMY* dressing, add 1 tsp.
guar or xanthan gum, mix well (see p.22)

GREEN GODDESS DRESSING

1 sm. can anchovies
Handful of parsley
8 - 10 leaves fresh tarragon, or 2 teaspoons dried
2 cups *Basic Salad Dressing*

Blend in a blender until smooth, or chop really fine
& mix well. Shake before using.

NUT & SEED BUTTERS, SPREADS & MILKS

A 'butter' can be made out of any kind of seed or nut, or combination. Day 2: Almonds, pine & brazil nuts, sunflower seeds.
Use a seed/nut mill or grinder, coffee-bean grinder, blender, or a food processor (use the metal blade) to produce a fine flour, or *meal*. One cup of whole nuts or seeds yields about 1/2 cup of ground flour, or *meal*. See manufacturer's instructions.

NUT BUTTER: 1 cup meal blended with about 3 tablespoons of water or oil. Add sea salt to taste. Blend, or mix until smooth.

DIP OR SPREAD: Add liquid to butter recipe above to bring mixture to the desired consistency. Season to taste. Add chopped nuts or seeds as desired.

SAUCE OR SALAD DRESSING: Add liquid to desired consistency. Season to taste

NUT OR SEED MILK *(Designer Milks)*
1/4 cup nuts or seeds (see above) & 8 oz. water. Blend until smooth. Strain if desired. Add approximately 1 teaspoon honey **, raisin juice or fruit juice concentrate if desired. Use as a milk substitute.

Note: Do NOT give honey to an infant under one year of age, due to chance of botulism poisoning.

The flavor of butters, dips and spreads is improved by roasting the nuts or seeds slightly before grinding them. Half raw and half roasted is best - retains more nutritional value.

GUACAMOLE

Avocados contain the good kinds of fat & no cholesterol

1 large very ripe avocado
1 tomato chopped finely
1/8 cup lime juice
Chili powder to taste
Salt to taste (opt)

Mash avocado and mix with other ingredients. Use as a salad dressing or serve as a dip with tortillas or raw vegetables. Excellent with cooked, chopped seafood and garnished with lots of fresh greens.

Hint - Quick and easy avocado cubes: cut in two lengthwise, remove pit. Hold half in one hand - cut side up - and using a butter knife - *not a sharp knife* - **carefully** make 1/2" cubes by inserting the tip of the knife till you reach the skin. Slice in one direction and then the next. Gently squeeze the bottom of the skin and the cubes pop out. Use a spoon to scoop out any precious morsels clinging to the skin. Add to soups, salads, dips. I love to add them to refried beans. YUM!

Hint Sprinkle with a little lemon or lime juice - keeps them fresh and green - prevents untimely browning.

MARINATED VEGGIES

Double this recipe, it keeps well
1/3 cup lime juice
1 teaspoon dried seasonings: black pepper, bay leaf,
  dill, parsley, celery seed or cumin
1/2 cup safflower, corn or avocado oil
1 lb. (total) vegetables: parsnips, celery, eggplant,
peppers, bamboo shoots, Jerusalem artichokes,
  sweet potatoes.
  May use frozen veggies right out of the package
1/2 teaspoon salt

In a small saucepan combine lime juice and herbs;
simmer very gently for about 5 minutes; add oil. Cover
and set aside to steep. Cut vegetables into bite-sized
pieces. Hard vegetables such as parsnips, Jerusalem
artichokes, bamboo shoots, or egg plant may be lightly
steamed first, while others such as bell peppers, celery,
tomatoes, are best if left raw. Bite sized pieces of left-
over meats are delicious marinated. Toss vegetables,
etc. with salt in a large bowl. Fresh herbs make a nice
addition at this point. Pour marinade evenly over the
vegetables and toss again. Let sit at least 1 hour, best
overnight, to develop full flavor. Toss from time to time to
mix marinade with veggies, or marinate under pressure
by placing a weighted dish on top of them inside the
bowl.

Hint - Marinated veggies can be mixed into salads,
served as pickles or an appetizer. They make a nice
salad and delicious accompaniment to main dishes.
Refrigerate for up to 5 days, the flavor continues to
develop with age.

AVOCADO MOUSSE

2 tablespoons unflavored gelatin
  (see p 22 for substitutions)
1/2 cup cold water
1/2 cup boiling water
3 cups avocado, mashed
  (about 5 very ripe avocados)
3 stalks finely chopped celery
1/2 teaspoon celery powder or salt
1 teaspoon salt
1/2 cup *basic salad dressing*
Dash of Tabasco to taste
Fresh, crisp salad greens

Soak gelatin in cold water for 5 minutes. Add boiling water, stir to completely dissolve. Combine with remaining ingredients in blender & mix well. Pour the mixture in a quart mold which has been sprayed with non-stick coating. Chill until firm.

Serve on a bed of salad greens.

Hint - To unmold gelatin dishes "intact" - dip bottom half of mold in a pan of hot water for about half a minute, then place a flat, upside-down plate on top of mold and quickly turn right-side-up. Ta-Dah --.

Tuck fresh greens around the edges, add tomato wedges, radish roses, etc.

CRAB & AVOCADO SALAD

Great company dish   *Yield: 6 portions*
                                  Preheat Oven: 350°

1/2 lb. crabmeat (or shrimp)
1/3 cup celery, chopped
3 hard boiled duck eggs, chopped
   (sub 1/2 cup coarsely chopped nuts, or increase
   crab/shrimp to 1 lb.)
2 tablespoons pimiento, chopped
1/2 teaspoon salt (opt)
1/2 cup *basic salad dressing*
3 large avocados, whole
Lime juice
Salt to taste
1/2 cup finely chopped cashews or pistachios

Mix crabmeat, celery, eggs, pimiento, salt and salad
dressing together. Cut unpeeled avocados lengthwise in
half. Remove pits. Brush halves with lime juice and
sprinkle lightly with salt.

Fill avocados with crabmeat mixture. Spoon nuts over
crabmeat filled avocados. Place in a baking dish and
bake in a 350° oven for 10 minutes.

Hint - Serve as an appetizer, or as a main attraction,
along with a large tossed salad or with a large bowl of
soup and corn bread.

MARINATED SALMON SALAD

1 lb. firm fish (canned fish is OK)
1/4 cup *basic salad dressing*
1/4 cup celery, chopped
1 ripe avocado, cut up
1 can bamboo shoots
1 bell pepper, diced fine
1 chopped tomato
1 teaspoon seasoning - fennel, celery seed,
  cilantro or cumin.
Salt to taste

Poach, drain and chill fish (See instructions, p.). Cut fish into bite-sized cubes, mix with the other ingredients and marinate at least 1 hour before serving.

Serve on crisp romaine leaves, or use to stuff tomatoes or bell peppers.

MOLDED SEAFOOD SALAD

1 tablespoon unflavored gelatin
1/4 cup cold water
1/2 cup boiling water
3/4 cups *basic salad dressing*
1/2 cup diced celery
1 chopped tomato
1/2 green pepper, minced
1/2 teaspoon salt
1-1/2 cups cooked seafood, chopped or flaked
2 tablespoons pimentos, chopped

MOLDED SEAFOOD SALAD, con't --

Soak gelatin in cold water to soften, dissolve in hot water. Mix with dressing, combine with the remaining ingredients. pour in mold and chill until firm.

Hint- To unmold gelatin dishes "intact" - dip bottom half of mold in a pan of hot water for about half a minute, then place a flat, upside-down plate on top of mold and quickly turn right-side-up. Ta-Dah --. Tuck fresh greens around the edges, add tomato wedges, radish roses, etc.

HEARTY RABBIT SALAD

Good with any type of cooked meat or seafood

1/2 cup safflower, corn or avocado oil
1/3 cup lime juice
1 teaspoon dill weed
1/4 teaspoon salt
1/4 teaspoon tarragon
1 cup chopped celery
3/4 lb. shrimp, or any cooked, diced seafood or meat
2 cups cooked barley (sub any whole grain)
2 tomatoes, cut into wedges
1 cup chopped cashews or pistachios

Toss together gently all ingredients except the tomatoes and nuts. Cover and chill several hours.

Hint- Just before serving gently toss again, then top with tomatoes and nuts.

CREAMY CASHEW SOUP

Indulge yourself, you'll love it

2 cups cashews
4 cups water
3 tablespoons safflower or corn oil
Grated peel of 1 or 2 limes
Seeds from 2 to 3 cardamom pods
Salt to taste

Combine all ingredients in a blender.
until smooth, pour mixture into a medium sized
saucepan. Cover and simmer very gently, stirring
often, for 1/2 hour.

CLAM - AVOCADO SOUP

Quick, easy & delicious !

1-12 oz. can of clam juice
1 cup cashew meal or 1/2 cup cashew butter)
1/2 medium avocado

Combine the can (or bottle) of clam juice with
cashew meal or butter. Mix well and serve with
diced avocado floating on top.

PEASANT VEGETABLE SOUP

6 celery stalks, thinly sliced
1 bell pepper, chopped
2 tablespoons safflower or corn oil
8 cups water
1 cup each:
  chopped parsnips, eggplant, Jerusalem artichokes,
  bamboo shoots, and/or tomatoes.
1/4 cup barley, oats or corn
Salt to taste (always optional)
1 tsp. seasoning: chili, bell peppers, fennel, celery
  seed or leaves, cilantro or cumin.

Sauté celery, parsnips, and peppers in oil. Add the
water, seasonings and remaining vegetables; cook
covered over low heat for 30 minutes or until the grain is
done, & /or vegetables are tender. Add salt.

Hint - Flavor improves with time. Prepare early in the
day, refrigerate and reheat when hungry.

Hint - Get out of the kitchen!
Soups and stews are a snap to prepare in a crock
pot/slow cooker. Just need to plan ahead. See pages
147 and 164 for instructions and lots of ideas.

SEAFOOD BOUILLON

Good Basic Stock - Make Now, Use Later

2 lbs. fish trimmings (see p.168 - 170)
2 quarts water
1 tsp. seasonings, choose from:
   chili, bell peppers, fennel, celery seed
   & leaves, cilantro, cumin.
1 Tbsp. safflower or corn oil.
3 stalks celery, chopped
1 large bell pepper, chopped
2 teaspoons salt

Sauté celery and peppers in oil until soft, combine with remaining ingredients and simmer for about 1 hour; strain. This makes a good basic stock. It can be made ahead and stored in the refrigerator, or frozen.

Notes:

CASHEW VEGETABLES

4 cups any vegetable -
   parsnip, celery, eggplant, bell peppers,
   bamboo shoots, Jerusalem artichokes, sweet potatoes.
1 tablespoon safflower or corn oil
1/4 cup chopped cashews or pistachios
Salt to taste (opt)

Cut into bite-sized pieces. Cook vegetables until tender
but crisp. Drain. Heat oil in skillet. Add chopped nuts and
stir until sizzling. Add vegetables and gently heat
through. Season to taste.

SPICED EGGPLANT   Yield: 4 portions

2-1/2 cups peeled, diced, uncooked eggplant
1-1/2 cups diced celery
1 diced bell pepper
2 Tbsp. safflower, corn or avocado oil
1 diced tomato
2 tsp. seasonings: chili powder, fennel, celery seed &
leaves, cilantro or cumin & *Dash* of cayenne
1/2 teaspoon salt
1 tablespoon lime juice

Brown eggplant and celery in medium sized saucepan.
Add 3/4 cups water and the remaining ingredients.
Cover and simmer over low heat 10 to 12 minutes or
until the water has evaporated and vegetables are
tender.

VEGGIE BURGER Dujour #4

1/2 cup celery, chopped
1/2 finely chopped bell pepper
1/2 cup cashews or pistachios, chopped
1/4 cup tapioca flour, or egg or egg substitute
2 tablespoons safflower, corn or avocado oil
1/2 teaspoon salt, if desired
2 cups cooked, mashed Jerusalem artichokes,
  or sweet potatoes

Combine all ingredients. Shape into patties. If too dry, add water; if too moist, add flour or nut meal to desired consistency. Sauté patties in lightly oiled skillet until browned nicely on both sides.

Hint - Great for a breakfast change!

Hint - This is a wonderful, versatile patty. Travels well, easy to pack and take in the car, or to school, or to work, or traveling.

Easy to mass-produce in advance. Make up several ahead of time and freeze for future use.

NUTTY LOAF

Preheat Oven: 350°

3 cups cashews &/or pistachios
1/4 cup psyllium seed, ground
1/4 cup water
1 cup finely chopped celery
1 cup finely chopped bell peppers
1 tsp. seasoning, choose from:
 anise, caraway, chervil, dill seed & dill weed, finely
 chopped pimento, dash of cayenne

Grind nuts in blender or food processor. Mix flax seed
and 1/4 cup of water - let stand until it reaches the
consistency of an egg. Combine remaining ingredients,
mix well. Place in a well oiled loaf pan and bake for 25
minutes at 350°.

CREAMY SAUCE

1/2 cup ground cashews or pistachios
2 cups water
2 tablespoons ground psyllium seed
1 tsp. of above seasoning
Dash of cayenne pepper
1/2 teaspoon salt (optional)

Combine all ingredients, mix well in small saucepan,
bring to simmer, (stir constantly) reduce heat, simmer
over low heat until thick. Pour over cooked loaf. Serve
hot.

Hint- Use the sauce like gravy. Pour it over any
cooked grain, starchy vegetable, etc.

NUTTY STUFFED TOMATOES

Yield: 6 portions

3/4 cup cashews or pistachios, chopped
6 large tomatoes (3 lbs.)
1 teaspoon salt
1 cup parsley, chopped
1/2 cup celery, chopped
1/4 cup pimiento, chopped
1/8 cup safflower, corn or avocado oil
1/4 cup lime juice
Dash cayenne pepper
1 tsp. dill weed or fennel seed
Lettuce leaves
Lime wedges

Slice off the stem end (top) of the tomatoes; core. Scoop out center over bowl, leaving a firm shell. Sprinkle inside of shells with salt; invert on paper toweling for 30 minutes to drain. Meanwhile, chop up the tomato pulp and mix with all remaining ingredients, except lettuce and lime wedges, toss gently.

To assemble - spoon nut mixture into tomato shells, mounding slightly. Garnish with additional chopped nuts if desired.

Arrange on lettuce lined salad platter. Sprinkle with sprouts if you like. Fresh sprouts are a nice addition to the filling, also.

Hint - Prepare early in the day, refrigerate until serving.

SLOW (CROCK POT) COOKING

Breakfast can be a snap when you know how to get a head start.

Lightly oil *or spray*, inside of pot to prevent sticking.
Add:
1 cup whole grains: barley, oats, spelt, teff or kamut.
2 cups water
1/2 cup cut-up, dried peaches, bananas, mangos, pitted
   cherries, blueberries or coconut.
Pinch of salt (optional)

Stir. Turn on low before retiring. In the morning, sweeten with maple syrup (if desired), &/or add nut milk and enjoy.

Hint - After breakfast, empty the pot and start dinner:
Place a cut-up rabbit, turkey parts or duck in the pot, add 2 cups water, cut-up parsnips, celery, bell peppers, eggplant or sweet potatoes. Turn heat on High. Dinner will be ready by 5 PM.

Can't have grain?
Try this procedure for cooking meat or poultry:
Place meat in pot before bedtime without vegetables. Have the meat for breakfast, pack some to take in your lunch. Then place the vegetables in the pot, on top of the meat, and let simmer on *low* heat until lunch or dinner time.

Want more ideas? See p.164, *cooking whole grains*.

FISH WITH A K.I.S.S. Yield: 6 portions

1/4 cup safflower, corn or avocado oil
3 tablespoons cashews or pistachios, chopped
2 lb. fish fillets
1 tablespoon grapefruit or lime juice
1/2 teaspoon dill weed or parsley
Dash of cayenne

Heat 2 tablespoons of oil in a large skillet. Add nuts and sauté over a medium heat 2 to 3 minutes until golden brown, stirring constantly. Remove nuts and set aside. In remaining oil, cook fish 3 to 4 minutes on each side until fish flakes when pierced with a fork. Remove to a warm platter and season with salt and pepper. Stir remaining ingredients into pan drippings with nuts and spoon over fish.

Hints - **Even more simple;**
Sprinkle fish with tasty topping, sauté until tender.

Like it crispy?
Sprinkle with tasty topping, coat with ground cashews or pistachios, bake or fry until golden brown.

Or - try this...
Baked fillets: Rinse fish, place in greased baking dish. Sprinkle with tasty topping or the above seasonings, bake in preheated hot oven (400 F) about 20 minutes.

Serve with tossed green salad, sliced tomatoes, steamed vegies and/or baked sweet potato.

RICH RABBIT STEW

Yield: 8 portions
Preheat Oven: 300°

1 lb. ground rabbit (sub any poultry)
1/2 cup bell peppers, chopped
1/2 cup celery, chopped
4 cups thickly sliced parsnips &/or eggplant
3 cups tomatoes
1/2 teaspoon salt
1 cup barley (optional)*
1/2 cup chopped cashews or pistachios.
Season to taste

Brown meat with celery and peppers, add eggplant or parsnips and place in a 2 quart baking dish. Add tomatoes, salt, barley* and seeds or nuts. Bake at 300° for 1 hour or until barley* and parsnips are tender.

Hint - If barley is not tolerated in your diet, replace by increasing cashews or pistachios to 1-1/2 cups.

Hint - Instead of baking - this casserole may also be prepared by simmering over a low heat in a heavy pan with a tight cover for 45 minutes or use a crock pot.

Notes:

CRISPY CASHEW RABBIT

Yield: 6 portions
Preheat Oven: 375°

1/2 cup tapioca flour
1 teaspoon salt
1/8 teaspoon pepper
1 teaspoon paprika
1 rabbit, cut-up, about 2-1/2 lbs.
2 tablespoons tapioca flour
6 tablespoons water
1 cup cashews, finely chopped
2 tablespoons safflower, corn or avocado oil
Salt to taste

Mix arrowroot, salt, pepper and paprika together, coat cut up rabbit pieces with mixture. Combine arrowroot starch and water - moisten the rabbit pieces with the mixture, then coat them with finely chopped cashews and place in a shallow baking pan.

Drizzle oil over rabbit pieces and sprinkle lightly with additional salt if desired. Bake at 375° for 30 minutes. Turn and then bake an additional 40 minutes longer until rabbit is tender and well browned.

CRACKERS & PIE CRUSTS

Made From Flour:

2 cups tapioca, barley, oat, corn or wheat flour
1 teaspoon baking powder or soda
1 teaspoon salt (opt.)
1/3 cup safflower, corn or avocado oil
1/3 cup cold water (approximate measure)

Made From Nuts Or Seeds:
2 cups cashew or pistachio meal (see p.27)
1 tsp. baking powder
1 tsp. salt (opt)
1/3 cup thickener (tapioca, ground psyllium seed,
   agar agar or *flour* above)

Hint- Oil is not usually needed with nuts and seeds. If finished product is too hard, add 1/8 cup oil next time.

Combine flour, baking powder or soda and salt. After mixing well, add oil or fat and mix with a fork until crumbly. Add water slowly, as needed, form into 2 balls. Chill thoroughly.

Notes:

Place ball on lightly greased baking sheet, roll out to about 1/4" thick. Dust dough with flour as necessary to keep from sticking to rolling pin, cut into 2" squares. Prick with fork all over. Bake in middle of preheated oven 350° for 10 minutes or until brown. (Time varies depending on type of flour used.) Watch carefully to prevent burning.

Hint- Cut Fun Shapes with cookie cutters, make diamonds, stripes, hearts, circles or whatever.

Herbal munchies: Add to mixture 1/2 tsp. seasoning, choose from: chili powder, dried bell peppers, fennel, celery seed, cilantro or cumin.

Save Crumbs from broken and odd-shapes, crumble and use for cracker or bread crumbs, for croutons, stuffings, etc.

Just for fun: Sprinkle with chopped nuts, seeds, coconut or finely chopped dried fruit, and roll again before cutting into squares.

Pie Crust:
Roll out and place into pie pan, or place ball in pan and press into place, flute edge as desired. Prick with fork. Bake at 350° for approximately 15 minutes, cool and add filling. Chill before serving.

PANCAKES made from flour

1-1/2 cups flour (barley, oat, or corn - if tolerated)
1/4 teaspoon salt
1 tablespoon baking powder
1 egg (or substitute, see p.23)
1-3/4 cups liquid: nut milk - cashew or pistachio, or juice
- peach, cherry, grapefruit, tangerine
1/8 cup safflower, corn or avocado oil

Combine dry ingredients and mix well. Combine egg, liquid, oil; add to dry ingredients. Bake on preheated, non-stick griddle, turn when browned and bubbly.

Hint- If batter thickens, add small amounts of liquid as needed. Cool on wire rack so they don't stick together.

Double the Recipe: Use extras as a bread substitute.

Great for Lunches:
Make multi-layered sandwiches, or spread with fillings and roll them up jelly roll fashion (like crepes or burritos).

Use your imagination for fillings, anything goes. (See lunch suggestions).

PANCAKES made from nuts or seeds

1&1/2 cups nut meal - cashew or pistachio
  plus 1/2 cup tapioca or other thickener, see p.26
1 teaspoon baking powder or soda
1 teaspoon salt (optional)
1/3 cup liquid: nut milk - cashew or pistachio or juice -
  peach, cherry, grapefruit - tangerine)
1/4 cup safflower, corn or avocado oil
1 egg or substitute (see p.23)

Combine dry ingredients together and mix well.
Combine nut milk and egg and blend together with dry
ingredients, mixing gently. Bake on pre-heated, non-
stick griddle.

Hint - If batter thickens, add small amounts of liquid as
needed. Cool on wire rack so they don't stick together.

Double the Recipe: Use extras as a bread substitute.

Great for Lunches:
Make multi-layered sandwiches, or spread with fillings
and roll them up jelly roll fashion (like crepes or
burritos).

Use your imagination for fillings, anything goes. (See
lunch suggestions).

Kid Pleasers:
Build multi-level sandwiches with a variety of fillings, or
spread with filling and roll up jelly-roll fashion like
crepes or burritos

WONDERFUL WAFFLES *made with flour*

1-1/2 cups flour (barley, oat, or corn - if tolerated)
1/4 teaspoon salt
1 tablespoon baking powder
1 egg (or substitute, see p.23)
1-3/4 cups liquid: nut milk - cashew or pistachio, or juice
- peach, cherry, grapefruit - tangerine
1/4 cup safflower, corn or avocado oil
1 tablespoon maple syrup (optional)

Combine dry ingredients , mix well. Combine egg, liquid,
oil and molasses together, mix and add to dry
ingredients.

Hint - Bake in **pre-heated,** greased or sprayed waffle
iron, *with a* **non-stick surface.** *This is important!
Heavy flours tend to stick.* Otherwise, you'll be scraping
off the waffle in bits and pieces, cursing me --- not a
good way to start the day.

WONDERFUL WAFFLES - *with nuts or seeds*

1-1/2 cups nut meal (cashew, or pistachio)
  plus 1/2 cup tapioca or other thickener, see p.26.
1 teaspoon baking powder or soda
1 teaspoon salt, (optional)
1/3 cup liquid: nut milk - cashew or pistachio, or juice -
  peach, cherry, grapefruit or tangerine
1/4 cup safflower, corn or avocado oil
1 egg or substitute (see p.23)

Use the same mixing and baking instructions as above.

NUTRI OLA

Cereal -- Breakfast Bar -- Snack Bar
Yield: 10 portions   Preheat Oven: 275°

2 cups finely ground barley, oats, corn, wheat or tapioca;
Or 2 cups finely ground cashews or pistachios
2 cups coarsely ground cashews or pistachios
Or 1 cup rolled oats or barley and 1 cup nuts
Note: You'll need 4 cups total of above ingredients.

1 cup ribbon or shredded coconut
1 cup finely chopped, dried peaches, mangos, bananas,
  or whole blueberries
1/2 cup maple syrup, sago palm, malt sweetener,
  concentrated fruit juice or fruit puree
1/8 cup oil (optional)

Preheat oven to 275°. Use a blender and or food processor to grind nuts, grains or seeds to desired consistency. Mix the nuts, seeds and/or grains in a large bowl. Mix together with fruit and sweetener, oil. Pour over the dry mixture and stir lightly. Spread mixture in a baking pan (15 x 10 x 1").

Bake for 1 hour stirring every 15 minutes. Cool

Break into small pieces for cereal or large chunks for snacks. Store in labeled container.

This recipe makes approximately 6 cups.

Nutri Ola Snack Bars

Add to basic recipe - 2 eggs (or egg substitute), slowly add additional liquid (water or juice) to make a stiff batter. Follow above directions, bake at 350 F about 30 minutes, cut into squares.

Hint- Taste batter before baking, make sure you like it. Add more sweetener or salt if desired.

BASIC MUFFINS

Preheat Oven: 350°
Yield: 12 lg. or 18 small* muffins

2 cups flour (barley, oat, or corn - if tolerated)
Or 1&1/2 cups nut meal - cashew or pistachio, plus
  1/2 cup tapioca flour
1 teaspoon baking powder
1/2 teaspoon salt (optional)
1 egg or substitute, see p.p.
1/3 cup safflower, corn or avocado oil
1 cup nut milk - cashew or pistachio, or juice - peach, cherry, grapefruit or tangerine

Sift dry ingredients together. Mix wet ingredients together well. Combine with dry ingredients, stirring until just blended, do not over beat. Fill greased muffin cups 1/2 full. Bake in preheated 400° oven for 12 to 15 minutes.

BLUEBERRY: Add 1 cup blueberries to batter.

BANANA NUT: Add 1 medium sized, ripe, mashed banana plus 1/2 cup chopped cashews or pistachios.

Hint- *To avoid dreaded soggy middles,* use small (tiny) muffin tins.

HEAVENLY NUT BREAD - #4

Moist and wonderful!   Pre-heat oven 350°F.

2 cups flour (barley, oat, or corn - if tolerated)
Or 1 & 1/2 cups nut meal - cashew, or pistachio, plus
   1/2 cup tapioca or other thickener, see p.26
1-1/2 teaspoons baking soda
1/2 teaspoon salt, if desired
1/2 teaspoon cinnamon
1/2 cup chopped cashews or pistachios
1/8 cup safflower, corn or avocado oil (opt.)
1 cup pure maple syrup, malt syrup, or fruit puree
1 cup liquid; nut milk - cashew or pistachio, or
   juice - peach, cherry, grapefruit or tangerine
3 eggs or substitute, see p.23
1-1/2 cups sweet potato (cooked and pureed)
1-1/2 teaspoons vanilla

Combine dry ingredients together and mix well.
Combine wet ingredients together and mix well.
Gradually and gently blend wet and dry ingredients
together. Batter will be very thick. Spread in oiled and
floured pans and bake at 350° for about 1 hour until a
knife or toothpick inserted in the middle comes out
clean.

BLUEBERRY NUT BREAD:
Omit sweet potato and fold in 1 cup blueberries after
batter is mixed,

BANANA NUT BREAD:
Substitute 2 ripe, mashed bananas for the sweet potato.

NUT BUTTER COOKIES

Quick to fix - an all-time favorite
Preheat Oven: 350° Yield: 2-1/2 doz.

1 cup nut butter - cashew or pistachio
1/2 cup pure maple syrup, sago palm, or coconut syrup
   or fruit puree
1/4 cup safflower, corn or avocado oil
1/4 teaspoon salt (optional)
2 cups flour- (barley, oat, or corn -
Or 2 cups nut meal - cashew or pistachio, plus
   1/2 cup tapioca flour
Or 2 cups tapioca or other thickener, see p.26

Preheat oven to 350°. Stir nut butter, sweetener, flavoring and oil together until smooth. Stir dry ingredients together; then mix with batter - a little at a time.

Hint - *Mix flour in with hands, not an electric mixer!*

Mix well. Roll dough into 1" balls, place on oiled cookie sheet, flatten with a fork.

Or form into rolls on waxed paper. Chill and slice 1/2" thick.
Bake for about 10 minutes, watch closely to avoid burning. Makes 2-1/2 dozen
Uncooked dough keeps well in refrigerator. Slice as needed. Freezes nicely also.

The following two recipes - **"uncandies"** - require no cooking - keep well - are great for snacks any time of the day and are excellent travelers

PEACHY - CASHEW BARS

2 cups dried fruit - peach, pitted cherries, nectarine, mango
2 cups nut or seed meal - cashew or pistachio
1/4 teaspoon salt (optional)
1/2 teaspoon vanilla

Food Processor: Cut fruit into small pieces, toss into the food processor; add nuts or seeds, salt and vanilla, blend until ball forms. Use the metal chopping blade.
Blender: Cut up fruit, place in blender and chop fine. Chop nuts separately, mix with fruit. Use sturdy spoon to mix and knead, or use fingers. If too dry to mix well, a small amount of water or juice. Batter will be *very* stiff **Press** firmly into oiled pie pan or cookie sheet, cut in squares; or place on waxed paper; form into 2" roll - or in little balls - roll in additional chopped nuts or seeds; . Wrap logs in waxed paper or foil (shiny side next to food). chill and slice as needed. Store in refrigerator.

CASHEWY uncandy *CANDY*

1 cup nut butter - cashew or pistachio
1/4 cup pure maple syrup, or to taste
1/2 cup shredded coconut
1/2 cup chopped nuts - cashews or pistachios

Toss into food processor; or use sturdy spoon to mix. Follow the above directions -- starting with ***Press** firmly-*

Helpful Hints
for both the
Novice and Experienced Cook

Basic Cooking Instructions
for
Beans, Grains, Poultry, Fish

How & Why To Clean Foods

Time-Saving Crock Pot Cookery

Deluxe Combo Collection - recipes
for parties or entertaining

Table of Contents

HOW TO *REALLY* CLEAN FOODS

You can react to a chemical, preservative or mold - on or in a food - and think that you are reacting to the food itself. Thorough cleaning allows you to be *almost* certain that if you experience a negative reaction, you are reacting to that food, and not an unseen, unwanted substance. So - In order to reduce the chance of an adverse reaction, clean foods as best you can, using one of the following methods.

Ponder this - How many people handle your food before it gets to your table? Think about the field workers and produce people who harvest or display the food you are eating. After using the toilet, cleaning their noses or smoking, do they *always* wash their hands with warm soapy water? Is it always available for them?

Organically grown foods are the best bet, the most nutritious and void of pesticides. Even though organically grown foods are pretty 'clean', they may be dirty or moldy. Molds are naturally present in or on most foods, removing as much as possible may prevent adverse reactions.

If you don't use the Clorox soak, scrub all fruits and vegetables with soap and water, then rinse well. Peeling root vegetables may remove some of the mold, but it also just spreads it around, so scrub before peeling.

Melons and root vegetables especially need to be cleaned. When we cut into the melon the blade drags hidden mold into the flesh of the melon; the same applies to squash and pumpkins. I am sensitive to these molds, and tolerate foods much better after using the liquid bleach soak.

CLOROX SOAK -

Step #1:
1 tsp. liquid Clorox to 2 gallons of water (use the Clorox brand only). Place fresh fruits, vegetables, meat or fish in the bath. Soak 20 minutes for heavy skinned foods and 15 minutes for most other foods.

Step #2:
Drain. Add fresh water and soak another 15 minutes. Drain again.

Step #3:
After draining, wrap in paper towels or a clean cloth (a piece of an old sheet is ideal), place in storage bag and refrigerate.

Antibiotics are usually added to the ice that fish is packed in when caught, so it is important to use the soak or at least to rinse fish well under running water before cooking.

Alternative cleaners: If the Clorox smell doesn't agree with you, add 1/4 cup baking soda or 1/4 cup of vinegar to the rinse water instead. Shaklee's *Basic H*, or Nutri Biotic's *Citricidal* liquid are worth trying, also. Shop around. There are several brands of unscented, non-toxic cleaners on the market.

Wilted vegetables get crisp and the flavor improves.

Thanks to the late James Shea, MD for this formula.

SLOW (CROCK POT) COOKING

Get out of the Kitchen and still cook from scratch. *My "pot" is always working for me. It's either cooking some sort of fruit sauce, bean dish, or soup - depending on the season and/or my activities.*

Simply place the food in a crock pot, and plug it in. The "unwatched pot" cooks slowly without the need for constant stirring and fussing - and the temperature is controlled so that the food never spoils nor scorches.

• Breakfast can be a snap by starting it before bedtime. Whole grains cook all night and are ready to eat on rising.

• Start dinner in the morning before leaving the house and come home to a hot, healthy meal of 'safe' food.

• Place a turkey hindquarter, pot roast, stewing hen, rabbit or whatever, in the pot at 10 p.m. and have tender, juicy breakfast ready at 6 a.m. After breakfast, toss some vegetables of the day into the pot, on top of the meat, and let simmer until lunch or dinner time.

• Old Fashioned Bean Soup, Chili or Split Pea Soup can be hot and ready to eat at any time of the day or night -- without fuss or muss. They hardly even need to be stirred.

Read the booklet that comes with the pot for additional ideas and time saving hints. See colored pages - days 1, 2, 3 and 4 - for additional ideas and specific meal plans.

COOKING WHOLE GRAINS

General Directions:
Whenever possible, use whole, unprocessed grains -
such as brown rice instead of white rice - since most of
the nutritional value and fiber is lost in the hulling and
polishing of grains. Rinse grain in cold water to remove
dust, dirt and talc.

> • Water to grain ratio is usually 2:1
> *2 cups water to 1 cup grain*

Rub a small amount of oil in the pot to prevent sticking.
Add grain to cold water, bring to boil, reduce heat, cover
and simmer for:

> • 20 to 30 minutes for small or soft grains like
> amaranth, barley, buckwheat groats, millet,
> oats, quinoa, spelt or teff

> • 45 minutes for brown rice, kamut or rye

Cook until bubbling stops and a slight crackling begins.
Try to avoid looking into the pot so that the steam won't
escape.

Salt is always optional; it may be added before
(preferably) or after cooking.

• When using a pressure cooker, follow manufacturer's
directions.
• Refer to crockpot cooking for the simplest preparation of
grains and beans.

COOKING DRIED BEANS & PEAS

Basic Directions:

Ratio of water to beans should be 3:1
   3 cups of water to 1 cup of beans.

Rinse, sort and search for clumps of dirt. To reduce cooking time cover with water, soak overnight.

Quick Soak:
Bring to boil, let stand 2 hours, continue cooking.

After soaking, bring to boil, reduce heat and simmer for a long, long time, as long as possible - at least twice as long as the directions call for. The longer beans cook, the easier they are to digest, and you'll have less gas and indigestion. All day is not too long.

Add water as needed during cooking, don't salt until almost done.

Hint - In a hurry? Use a pressure cooker. Pressure cookers speed cooking time for beans, dried peas or lentils. Follow manufacturer's directions.

Hint - Reward yourself for planning ahead: Use a crockpot for the simplest, hassle-free cooking of beans.

See *Day 1 and Day 3* sections for recipes, See *crock pot cooking* in each colored section for specific suggestions and recipes; and page 164 for some more tips.

COOKING BEANS, con't

How to set up a simple "bean routine"

Step #1 - Let's say, for instance, you've had lima beans on Monday - Day 1; at the end of the day empty the pot, place the beans in freezer containers; identify the containers as Day 1 with a green sticker or green rubber band, place on green shelf in freezer for a future 'Day 1' meal.

Step #2 Wash and sort the type of bean you want on Day 3, place in pot and cook on low until Wednesday-Day 3. At the end of Day 3, empty the pot and repeat

Repeat Step #1: Place Day 1 beans in the pot and cook on low until Friday. You can have the pot working full-time for you.

When you get the hang of this, and have set up and easy routine - purchase a second pot and enjoy hot, ready- to-eat soups or stews throughout each and every day.

Hint - Cook 4 times the amount you need and freeze them for use later. They thaw easily and make wonderful bean dips, refried beans, humus, burritos and salads. (See recipes).

Note: Monday won't always be Day 1, this is just an example.

FRESH FISH IS GOOD FOR YOU

Fish Types and the Best Ways to Cook Them

Helpful Hint: For those of you who are rotating your foods - you can have fish daily - as long as you choose a *different* fish each day.

Cod has a mild flavor and firm, white flesh. Prepare it by any of the basic cookery methods. It goes well with a variety of sauces.

Flounder and Sole have delicate flavors, flaky white meat and a moist, fine texture. Try them prepared in any of the basic methods.

Ocean Perch is a red-skinned fish with a flavor similar to freshwater perch and bass. Lean, full-flavored ocean perch will go in almost any of your favorite dishes.

Salmon, the five best known species of salmon vary in flesh color from almost white to characteristic bright red. Try them barbecued, poached, baked, broiled, steamed or served cold for salads.

Catfish has fine texture and excellent flavor. Deep fried catfish served with hush puppies is a favorite, but try catfish in a chowder or baste it with sesame seeds and butter and grill over hot coals.

Fish Types and the Best Way to Cook Them

Rainbow Trout makes a delightful and quick to fix, special meal. Fresh or frozen trout can be pan-fried, baked or barbecued on the grill. It is also wonderful stuffed or poached. Beware of the pesky, tiny little bones.

Red Snapper with it's firm, snowy white meat has a sweet flavor and faint pink cast. Fillets or steaks are particularly good broiled or baked. And, whole red snapper is delicious prepared with a stuffing.

Halibut is mild and wonderful! Good baked or poached. Try halibut steaks basted with a sauce or marinade and then broiled or grilled.

Notes -

A Quick & Easy FISH COOKING GUIDE

Timing
is the real secret of delicious fish cookery.
Here's a simple rule for timing the cooking of fish.

Measure the fish fillet or steak at its thickest part, then figure 10 minutes of cooking time per inch of thickness. If the fish measures less than 1", shorten the cooking time proportionately.

If the fish is frozen, double the cooking time to 20 minutes per inch of thickness. And, if you are going to cook the fish in foil or in a sauce, allow an extra 5 minutes per inch. Your fish will be done when the flesh becomes opaque and flakes very easily with a fork.

To Bake:
Place cleaned, dressed fish in a greased baking dish. Brush with butter, oil or sauce to keep it moist.

Lemon slices under the fish will add flavor and prevent sticking. Bake at 350°. Whole fish lend themselves well to baking as do fillets and steaks.

To Broil:
Select fillets, steaks or split sides. Arrange in a single layer on a well greased broiler rack. Keep fish 4" from the heat. Baste with melted fat or oil before, after and during broiling. Do not turn.

A Quick Guide to Cooking Fish, con't...

To Pan or Oven Fry:
Dip clean, dressed small fish or fish servings into beaten egg, or water, then into seasoned, finely ground nuts or seeds, bread crumbs, cornmeal or flour.

Pan Fry: Heat 2 TBSP or 1/8" oil in a pan. Place coated fish in a single layer in the hot oil. Turn once midway through the cooking.

Oven Fry: Place fish in a well greased shallow baking dish. Pour a little melted butter or margarine over the fish. Bake in a preheated 500° oven. Do not turn or baste.

To Poach:
Place liquid to barely cover a single layer of fish in a shallow wide pan such as a frying pan. Plain or seasoned broth, water or wine are several of the liquids that can be used. Bring liquid to a boil. Add fish, cover, reduce heat to *simmer* until done. Serve hot or cold.

To Steam:
Use a steamer or a shallow pan with a tight cover - deep enough to hold a wire basket or rack. Pour about 2" of water into the pot and bring to a rapid boil. Place fish on rack or basket, place in pot, keeping fish above the water. Cover pot tightly and steam until done.

Season the fish before steaming - dust with fresh or dried herbs. Thyme or dill are two of my favorites.

Basic Meat Roasting

Roast tender cuts of meat slowly; about 325°F; season with garlic, or other herbs, fresh or dried (don't salt yet), place fat side up on a rack in an open pan. Insert meat thermometer, in center of meat. Do not add water and do not cover. Roasted meat continues to cook after it has been removed from the oven

Due to the E Coli and other possible infectious organisms, it's better to over-cook, rather than under cook all types and cuts of meat.

Purchase organic meat from healthy animals from your natural foods store whenever possible. *If I ate meat, I wouldn't eat anything else but organically grown.*

Pre-heat oven 325°F.
Internal temperature should be;
140° for rare;
160° for medium;
170° for well done.

See section on *crock pot cooking* for ideas in preparing pot roasts, corned beef, and other less tender cuts of meat.

Notes:

Basic Poultry Roasting

All kinds of poultry including chicken, Cornish game hen, turkey, duck and goose are delicious roasted. Poultry can be roasted whole, either stuffed or unstudied.

Whole onions, chopped celery, and various other vegetables may be used instead of the traditional bread - type starchy stuffing. They add delightful flavor and moisture to the roasted bird.

Simply sprinkle with seasonings of your choice, place a few vegetables in the cavity and bake at 350° F about 1 hour for small birds. For turkeys, see produce's directions.

Easy, elegant one-dish meal:
Put 1 cup whole grain plus 2 cups water in roasting pan, spread evenly; place small birds or pieces of large birds on top, season and roast as usual. The juices from the bird drip into the grain and make a tasty one-dish meal.

Especially good with game birds on top of kamut, quinoa, wild or brown rice.

Notes:

BASIC POULTRY ROASTING, con't -

Plan the roasting time for a large bird so it will be done 20 to 30 minutes before you plan to serve it. It will be easier to carve after it has been allowed to stand for a few minutes.

How do I know when it's done?
The meat of the fleshy part of the drumstick feels soft when a bird is done. Or, you can tell if it is thoroughly cooked if the drumstick moves up and down easily, and the leg joint gives easily or breaks. A meat thermometer is your best bet with whole turkeys. To test for doneness place the thermometer in the inner thigh muscle of the turkey. When it reads 180° to 185°, the bird is done.

See section on `crock pot cooking' for additional time saving ideas

Deluxe Combo Section ---
The following recipes are a collection of my favorites - great for family gatherings, parties or entertaining. The ingredients are not coordinated with the Master Chart or the colored pages. They are simply healthy, delicious dishes for you to fix when you are bored with food and/or simply want a festive meal.

Notes:

BOUILLABAISSE

Seafood Stew - a great company dish

2 lbs. fish
1 quart water
1/8 cup oil
2 onions, chopped
1 clove garlic, crushed
1 teaspoon each thyme and fennel seeds
1 bay leaf
About 8 mussels & 8 clams
1 cup lobster meat
1 cup shrimp, shelled
1/2 cup pimentos, sliced
Tiny pinch of saffron

Simmer the 2 lbs. of fish until the water is reduced by half. Save the broth. Cut the fish into serving sized pieces. Place the oil in a heavy soup pan. Add onions, garlic and spices; sauté until soft. Add the broth and simmer for 5 minutes. Add the fish, mussels, clams, lobster meat, shrimp and pimentos. Simmer another 10 minutes.

Crumble saffron into soup and stir gently to distribute.

Serve with a large tossed salad, homemade crackers of the day, muffins or nut bread.

HEARTY ALASKA COD CHOWDER

Yield: 6 portions

1-1/2 lbs. Alaska cod fillets*
1 cup onion, chopped
1 cup zucchini, chopped
1 large clove garlic, minced
1/8 cup oil
1 16 oz. can tomatoes
2 cups tomato juice
1/3 cup water
3/4 teaspoon salt
3/4 teaspoon crushed basil leaves
dash hot pepper sauce (optional)

*Any firm fish may be substituted. Cut thawed or fresh fillets into large chunks. Sauté onion, zucchini and garlic in oil until soft. Add remaining ingredients and heat to boiling. Add cod, turn heat to low and simmer, covered about 10 minutes or until fish flakes easily when tested with a fork. This recipe may be halved or doubled.

Microwave Method: Cut cod into large chunks. Combine onion, zucchini, garlic and oil in 3-1/2 quart microwave dish. Microwave, covered on High for 4 minutes or until onion is tender. Add tomatoes, tomato juice and seasonings. Microwave, covered on High 4 minutes or until boiling. Add cod. Microwave, covered, on High 4 minutes. Stir and microwave, covered, on High 4 to 6 minutes longer or until cod flakes easily when tested with a fork.

NEW ORLEANS GUMBO

1/2 lb. shrimp
1 quart water
1 tablespoon oil
1 small onion, minced
1 clove garlic, minced
1 stalk celery, chopped
1 cup or 1 can cut okra
2 sprigs parsley, chopped
1/2 teaspoon thyme   1 bay leaf
1/2 cup rice or amaranth*
1 tablespoon thickener
1/4 cup water
1/2 pint oysters
1 teaspoon file powder
Dash of hot sauce (to taste)

Shell the shrimp, boil the shells 10 minutes. Discard the shells and add water to the broth to make 1 quart. Brown vegetables in oil and add with spices to the stock, mix well. Add rice or amaranth (if tolerated in your diet*), the starch of the day and 1/4 cup of water. Simmer 1/2 hour or longer. Add oysters and shrimp and cook gently until the oysters begin to curl. Add file powder just before serving.

*You may leave out the grain, and serve the gumbo over any cooked grain, noodle, pasta, potato, or sprouts that fit into your special diet, or what ever suits your fancy.

Hint - I like to substitute bean sprouts for noodles; or just eat it without the starch, as a soup.

SEAFOOD RAGOUT

Yield: 6 - 8 portions

2 lbs. white fish, thick fillets of snapper or cod
2 cups onions, sliced (optional)
2-1/2 cups carrot, strips
2 tablespoons oil, olive or sunflower
1/4 cup rice flour* (optional)
1 - 16 oz can tomatoes, diced and juice
1 cup water
2 teaspoons salt
6 whole peppercorns or 1/8 teaspoon pepper
1 bay leaf
1 tablespoon lemon juice
parsley (optional)

Thaw fish if frozen. Cut into 1-1/2 to 2" chunks. Cook onions in oil until tender but not brown.

Stir in rice*. Add tomatoes, water, salt, pepper and bay leaf. Bring to boil. Cover and cook slowly allowing about 10 minutes for each inch of thickness of the fish.

Sprinkle with lemon juice and parsley before serving.

*Any flour may be used - depending on your food tolerances and preferences.

MEXICANA FIESTA TURKEY

Yield: 12 portions
Preheat Oven: 325°

5 lbs. turkey breast, split
2/3 cup safflower oil
1/2 cup lime juice
1/2 teaspoon salt
1/4 teaspoon coarsely ground black pepper
1- 8 oz. can tomato sauce
Diced jalapeno peppers (to taste)
1 teaspoon chili powder
1/2 teaspoon ground cumin

Arrange turkey in a shallow pan and combine other ingredients and pour over the turkey to marinate. Cover and refrigerate at least 8 hours. Turn occasionally. Pour off marinade and use to baste turkey during roasting.

Roast turkey in a preheated 325° oven for 3 hours or until meat thermometer reaches an internal temperature of 180° to 185 degrees.

Serve with any cooked grain, baked squash or potato; tossed green salad; sliced, raw jicama sprinkled with lime juice, salsa and corn tortillas, if tolerated.

RUM BALLS

Rich, moist and tempting

1/2 cup walnuts
3/4 cups currants
1/4 cup dried apricots
2 teaspoons rum or rum flavoring
    (sub. brandy or almond extract)
1/2 teaspoon vanilla
1/2 cup coconut, grated

Place nuts and fruits in a food processor or grinder and process until the fruit is chopped and the mixture clings together in a large ball. Add the rum and vanilla and process a few seconds more. Form into small balls with your hands and roll in grated coconut or chopped nuts. These are exceptionally good and keep well.

You'll love these! If you what more of this 'uncandy candy' see the four similar recipes in the colored pages.

Notes:

KETCHUP -- or is it CATSUP?

Yield: 1-3/4 cups

1 12 oz. can tomato paste
1/2 cup lemon juice (or substitute)
1/2 cup water
1/2 teaspoon salt (optional)
1 teaspoon oregano
1/8 teaspoon cumin
1/8 teaspoon nutmeg
1/8 teaspoon pepper
1/2 teaspoon dry mustard
Dash garlic powder

Mix all ingredients together really well. A blender works best. Keep refrigerated.

SEAFOOD (COCKTAIL) SAUCE

To Ketchup recipe - increase lemon juice to 1 cup
Add 1 Tbsp. horseradish (or to taste).
Dash of Tabasco sauce if desired.

Hint: Is the blender too messy and too hard to clean? After emptying the blender, fill 1/2 full with warm water, add a squirt of dish soap, place on the blender base and blend until it's squeaky-clean (just a couple of minutes). It's self-cleaning! Ta - daa! Simply rinse well under the faucet, and turn upside-down to drip dry.

ZESTY BARBECUE SAUCE

1 tablespoon oil
1 medium onion, chopped
1 clove garlic
1 cup Ketchup (see prev. page)
1/2 cup water
2 tablespoons Worcestershire sauce
1/2 teaspoon salt (optional)
Dash of Tabasco
Dash of liquid smoke * (optional)

In a saucepan, cook onion and garlic in oil until tender. Stir in remaining ingredients. Simmer covered for 10 minutes. Refrigerate remaining sauce for use later.

Serving Suggestions: Use on your favorite meats. It is excellent on chicken, pork, hamburger, fish, nut loaves, veggie burgers, even tofu. Adds zip to a bean dish; makes for a wonderful, robust flavor change.

Hint - When barbecuing on a grill, to prevent scorching &/or turning black and tasteless - add sauce during the last half of cooking; or over a very low fire.

Hint -This is the last recipe in this book, but I'm writing others. Feel free to write to me, share what works for you, what are your needs? For a free newsletter, include a #10 S.A.S.E.

Dr. Sally Rockwell PO Box 31065 Seattle, WA 98103 (206) 547-1814 FAX 547-7696

TABLE OF CONTENTS

Section Six - Tidbits

Note - *Purchase the following products from a merchant in your area whenever possible - your local book store or natural foods store. If not in stock have them order from their book distributor. If that doesn't work, fill out the form below and forward it to me. Send a #10 S.A.S.E. for a free copy of my newsletter, Allergy Alert.*

Happy cooking!

Dr. Sally Rockwell's Allergy Relief
SELF-HELP FOR THE DIVERSIFIED ROTATION DIET

What Do I Do? • Where Do I Start?
What's Left To Eat?

• Insures patient compliance • Easy, flexible, simple • Fun
• Promotes family independence • Often imitated - never equaled
• Friendlier and more personal than a computer printout

- ## The Rotation Game - $15.95
  Colorful Master Chart • Visual Aids • Food Diary • Food family lists •
  Menus and Recipes • Helpful Hints • Step-by-step instructions •
  Hints for Hypoglycemics • Label Reading

- ## Rotated Allergy Recipes Book - $11.95
  Companion to the *GAME*. - Colored sections coordinate
  Recipes Free of all major allergens Match colors & start cooking

- ## Master Chart - See all 4 days at a glance. Colorful, $4.
  plastic coated chart; for refrigerator or wall. Free with the Game.

- ## Illustrated Guide Books $3.50 ea.
  #1. How to Start a Diversified Elimination Diet
  # 2. How to Use a Food & Symptom Diary - Begin to Rotate
  #3. Allergy-Free Baking Tips

- ## Audio Tapes - Instructions - encouragement - support.
  • *Overcoming Food Allergies.* $10.95 ea.
  • *Non-dairy Calcium & Nutrition for the Allergic Person*
  • Video - *What's Left To Eat?* Color-coding; Rotate; Food Diary
  & What to Eat. One picture is worth 1,000 words. $24.95

Dr. Sally Rockwell's Allergy Relief
SELF-HELP FOR THE DIVERSIFIED ROTATION DIET

• *New* - **Calcium Without the Cow** - $15.95

The only vegan, wheat & sugar-free, rotated recipes book to date.
Calcium-Rich & Dairy-Free - Over 100 recipes and 14 menu plans
(complete with nutrient analysis). Wheat & sugar-free; vegetarian; rotated &
coordinated with *The Game*; calcium content of over 1,400 Foods, spices &
milk substitutes, designer milks - & lots more --

• *Candida Control* $10.95 ea.

Book: *Coping With Candida Cookbook (Over 50,000 in print)*
        Sugar-Free, hypo-allergenic, low-carb recipes
Tape: *How to Control & Conquer Candida*

Allergy Relief - Starter Kits

#1 - *Basic Starter Kit:*
        • *The Rotation Game* - -
        • *Rotated Allergy Recipes Book* -
        • 3 Guide Books
        • Audio Tape - Overcoming Food Allergies.
                Special $45 - and - FREE shipping

2 - *Professional Starter Kit*
        Includes all of the above, plus Video -*Ideal for office
        viewing, training doctors, dietitians, office staff, technicians*
                Special: $68 - and - FREE shipping

Send ASAP: _____ Professional Kits $68.   _____
             _____ Patient Kits   45.   _____

All Products may be ordered separately, see following page -

Note - Purchase the following products from a merchant in your area whenever possible - your local book store or natural foods store. If not in stock have them order from their book distributor. If that doesn't work, fill out the form below and forward it to me.

Happy cooking!

All Products may be ordered separately, or in Money Saving Starter Kits - see previous page -

Game ____   _____
Recipe Book ____   _____
Coping W Candida ____   _____
Guide Books: #1 ___ #2 ___ #6   _____
Calcium w/o the Cow ____   _____
Tapes: Audio: Allergy Relief ___ Candida ___ Calcium ___   _____
            Video: What's Left to Eat? ___   _____
Allergy Alert newsletter - 1 yr. ___ 2 yr. ___   _____

S&H: 1st item - $4: + $1 for ea. add'l item   Total $ _____.___

All products guaranteed - prices subject to change

I have enclosed a check, MO or Visa/MC #   (US funds)

Name _____

Address:_____

_____ _____zip _____

Visa/MC _____exp: _____

To: Sally Rockwell, Ph.D. PO Box 31065 Seattle, WA 98103
        (206) 547-1814   FAX (206) 547-7696

RESOURCES
Allergy-free foods, supplies & services:
Free catalogue: Allergy Resources PO Box 444 Guffy, CO. 80820
(800) USE-FLAX FAX (719) 689-2303
For physician referrals, contact:
AAEM - American Academy of Environmental Medicine
4510 W. 89th St. Prairie Village, KS 66207 (913) 642-6062
Send $3 and a #10 SASE.
AAND American Association of Naturopathic Physicians
Send $5 to: 2366 Eastlake Ave E., #322 Seattle, WA 98103
AHMA Am Holistic Med. Assoc. 4101 Lake Boon Trail #201
Raleigh, NC 27607 (919) 787-5146
Diet Design PO Box 31065 Seattle, WA 98103 *Send a large , #10*
S.A.S.E & $3 for Dr. referrals, info on misc. & "odd" foods
GLACM Great Lakes Assoc of Clinical Medicine
1407 B, N. Wells St Chicago Il, 60610 (800) 356-2228
PAAS - Pan American Allergy Society. *Send a #10 SASE & $5 to*
PO Box 947 Fredericksburg, TX. 78624

Books:
This is a teeny sampling of the dozens on the market.
Bread Machine Baking for Better Health: Chace & Keane, Prima Publ.
Super Foods, Marge Jones - 2615 N 4th St #616
Coeur d'Alene ID 83814
The Yeast Connection & the Woman, Wm Crook, MD.,
Hotline Publ. PO Box 161132, Altamonte Springs, FL 32716
Feed Your Body Right, by Lendon Smith, MD. Learn how to
"neutralize" allergic reactions with Life Balance (503) 221-1779
Smith's latest book is: *How To Raise a Healthy Child*
Doris Rapp, MD has several helpful books and tapes.
Her latest book: *Is This Your Child's World?*
Video: *Environmentally Sick Schools*

Newsletters:
Allergy Alert, For a free copy of my newsletter send a S.A.S. #10
envelope to: PO Box 31065 Seattle, WA 98103
Allergy Hotline, 5329 Diplomat Circle, #28,
Orlando, FL . 32810. Sample newsletter, $2.
Changing Appetites, Recipes for Allergy-Free Cooking.
1825 San Andres, Santa Barbara, CA 93101
In order to make your life I little easier, I am continually creating
new resources. Send for a current brochure.